#2

	DATE DUE		
9-30-10			

ALSO BY SAM R. HAMBURG, PH.D.

Understanding Alcoholism and Problem Drinking
(with W. R. Miller and V. V. Rozynko)

WILL OUR LOVE LAST?

A COUPLE'S ROAD MAP

Sam R. Hamburg, Ph.D.

SCRIBNER

New York London Toronto Sydney Singapore

SCRIBNER
1230 Avenue of the Americas
New York, NY 10020

Designed by Brooke G. Koven
Text set in Fournier MT
Manufactured in the United States of America

1 3 5 7 9 10 8 6 4 2

Permissions are on page 237.

Library of Congress Cataloging-in-Publication Data
Hamburg, Samuel R.
Will our love last?: a couple's road map/Sam R. Hamburg
p. cm.
Includes bibliographical references.
1. Marriage. 2. Married people. 3. Love. 4. Interpersonal relations. I. Title.
HQ734.H2573 2000
306.81—dc21   99–047241

ISBN 0-684-86491-6

To Luba, Sue, Anna

Contents

Author's Notes

Privacy

I have taken care to protect the privacy of the people whose stories are told in this book. Names and other identifying details have been changed. In some instances, elements from several similar cases have been amalgamated into one story.

Who's Who

Over the years as a psychologist, I have not done many workshops or seminars. I don't generally talk to large groups of people. I talk with only one or two people at a time. That's what I've been imagining as I've been writing this book: just you, who are reading this book, or listening to your partner read it to you, and me—the two or three of us in a quiet room somewhere. And as I've been writing this book—talking to you—I've been listening hard for what you've been saying back to me.

As part of making this book sound as if we are talking, I have referred to your partner as "they" rather than as "he or she," because when we talk with each other that's what we do. If you were talking with me you wouldn't say, "When someone on the street comes up to me, and he or she asks me for spare change, I usually reach into my pocket and give him or her something." You would say, "When someone on the street comes up to me, and they ask me for spare change, I usually reach into my pocket and give them something," which would sound perfectly natural to both of us. And anyway, you know whether your partner is a he or she.

Acknowledgments

This book is the direct result of a conversation with Dr. Eugene H. Winkler, pastor of First United Methodist Church, The Chicago Temple. I had never seriously considered writing a self-help book. On the morning of the day I started writing this book—the day of that conversation—I had no idea I would write it.

Dr. Winkler had invited me to give a series of talks on marriage at his church. He and I met one day in September 1997 to talk about what I might say. At the end of the conversation Dr. Winkler said, "Sounds great. Why don't you write me an outline?" As soon as he left my office I started—only I don't do outlines. I simply started writing the text for the first talk. By the second page, I realized that I was writing a book. When I later told Dr. Winkler that I had written the book because of our conversation, he demurred and suggested that I owed the book not to him but to Someone Else. I am in no position to argue, but I thank Gene Winkler, from the bottom of my heart, for being at least the agent of Providence.

Speaking of agents of providence . . . my agent, Candice Fuhrman! I will always be grateful to Candice for taking me on and for her wise guidance ever since. Likewise, I will always be grateful to Susan Moldow, of Scribner, for seeing value in my project.

The book owes its present form to two friends who were among its earliest readers, Reverend Paul Walther and Father Thomas Aldworth. Paul identified a major problem in the presentation of what are now chapters 9, 10, and 11. Tom read the manuscript with great care, made extensive notes, pointed out the same problem, and in a sentence told me how to correct it. I will always be grateful to Paul and Tom for their help.

Other people who read all or part of the manuscript and made critical and helpful comments include Lonnie Barbach, Daniel J. Conti, Susan crane, Toni Del Bene, Violet Franks, Susan Gal, Alan S. Gurman, Arnold A. Lazarus, Brian Moore, Tim Mulder, David Siegman, and Rita P. Sussman. I thank them all for their time and attention, and for their ideas. I am especially indebted to Elsa Dixon for her many astute editorial comments and corrections.

It was my great good fortune to be assigned Jake Morrissey as my editor at Scribner. Working with him has been a pleasure, and I am grateful to him for reminding me that there is always room for improvement.

Gene Mackay has been called "one of the finest draftsmen alive," and his works can be found in museums. It is a privilege to have his beautiful drawings in my book.

I, and this book, have benefited from twenty years of conversations with Timothy J. O'Connell—conversations about literature, philosophy, science, and many other things in addition to psychology. Tim's mark is all over this book, in some places I can identify and in others I cannot.

Most of what psychotherapists know they have learned from their clients. My clients have given me so much. I can only hope that at least some of them feel they have received fair exchange.

Finally, thanks are due to all the musicians—from Emma Kirkby to Sonny Rollins to Stevie Wonder—whose gifts grace us with ecstasy.

WHAT ABOUT my wife? This book is her acknowledgment.

PART ONE

Marriage
and
Happiness

1

THE QUESTION: WHAT MAKES MARRIAGES HAPPY?

Mystified by Love

A young woman—call her Jane—sits on the couch in my consulting room. She is wearing a tailored wool suit and has the crisp, put-together look of the successful career woman that she is. Jane is distraught and tearful. Her long, straight hair sweeps across her face as she cries. Between her sobs, this is what she says:

> I don't know if I love Bob anymore. But why shouldn't I? He's the perfect person. He's handsome, thoughtful, polite, hard-working, successful. He's from a great family. I know I loved him in the beginning . . . I think. But now, after being married five years, it's different. And then this guy in the office, Jim. I know he's interested in me. And I'm so attracted to him, he's getting harder and harder to resist. He's not nearly as good-looking as Bob, yet when I'm around him—when I think of him—I get this sexual rush. And when we talk, I feel so in tune with him. I think I love him—but I shouldn't.

Like so many people, married or not, Jane is *mystified* by love. She knows how love feels, but she doesn't know what love is. She can't account for why it flowers in her heart and why it withers. Mystified as she is by love, she can't answer one crucial question—a question whose answer will determine the future course of her life: Am I with the Right Person?

Men and women in love are haunted by this question. You may be haunted by it right now. You know that most people's marriages are not happy. You know—we all know—the statistics: Half of all marriages break up. As for the other half, you know that many of those people are not happy. They're trapped inside their "intact" marriages. And what spooks you most of all is knowing that many of these unhappy people were passionately in love at the start—just as you may be right now.

But you also know that some people's marriages are happy, and stay happy for a very long time—forever. You've seen and read true stories about happily married couples—Paul and Linda McCartney, for example. You may even know a happily married couple or two yourself. You see that the people in these marriages seem to work together smoothly as a team. They seem to genuinely like each other and to enjoy each other's company. And if you know them well enough, they may have even confided to you that they enjoy each other in bed—even after having been together for many years. When we get married, we hope that ours will be one of those exceptional, happy marriages. What makes the difference between a happy and an unhappy marriage?

The message of this book, a message rather different from what you will find in other books about marriage, is that the key to a happy marriage is picking the right person in the first place—someone with whom you are deeply compatible. The aim of this book is to equip you to do that. But you cannot choose the right person without first understanding the pressures—on you and everyone else contemplating marriage—to choose the wrong person. And you will not be really motivated to choose the right person unless you understand exactly what compatibility is and why it is so important to the happiness of your marriage. By the time you finish the first part of this book, you won't be mystified by love anymore. You will understand exactly how love works—where love comes from, why it disappears, and the crucial role that compatibility plays in keeping love alive. Then you'll be ready to go on to the second part and use it to evaluate whether you and your partner are compatible enough to have lasting love.

The idea that compatibility is the key to happiness in marriage may surprise and confuse you because other books have claimed that other things are the key. What does make marriage happy? Let's round up the usual suspects.

Communication? Commitment? Hard Work?—Guess Again

These are the usual suspects, aren't they? You've read about them in magazine articles. If you've ever read a self-help book about marriage, you've definitely read about the key importance of communication, commitment, and hard work. If you've seen the authors of self-help books on television, you've heard them speak about it. Well-meaning people may have spoken to you personally about how important communication, commitment, and hard work are to happiness in marriage.

When we hear the same reasonable-sounding message repeatedly from experts and other people we have reason to trust, we tend to assume it's true. Often that is a safe assumption, but sometimes it isn't. When we look closely and critically at something we have taken for granted—evaluate the logic of the argument and the soundness of the facts—we sometimes discover that it is not as true as we had thought. Let's take that kind of close and careful look at the claim that communication, commitment, and hard work are the key to happiness in marriage.

Communication

Communication has become so identified with marriage and its problems that many couples come into my office and say, "We have a communication problem," instead of just saying, "We have a marital problem." They have learned this from marital therapists.

It so happens that the pioneers of modern marital and family therapy were communication-oriented. They thought that all sorts of psychological problems could be caused by pathological communication. For example, they thought that schizophrenia could result if a mother communicated in paradoxical and confusing ways that made it impossible for her child to understand what the mother wanted. One example of such a "double bind" is the command "Disobey me." If you disobey in response to that command, you are obeying!

Contemporary marital therapists don't think that bad communication can cause quite such devastating effects as schizophrenia but they do think that bad communication contributes greatly to marital problems. Accordingly, these therapists devote a lot of time to teaching couples how to communicate better. They train their clients to express their feelings more directly and listen to each other more sensitively, and they teach them techniques for handling conflict and for negotiating and problem solving.

It's a great advantage, in marriage, to have good communication and problem-solving skills. In happy marriages, these skills help partners express their love for each other, and they help day-to-day life run more smoothly. But when marriages are in trouble, it's not necessarily because the partners lack communication skills. Most people with marriage problems are perfectly good communicators. In fact, research has shown that spouses who have problems communicating with each other have *no trouble at all* communicating with anybody else.[1] And I have done marital therapy with scores of unhappily married lawyers, upper-level business executives, sales and marketing people, advertising and public relations people, and even writers. They all had wonderful communication skills; they were all ace problem solvers. Not being able to communicate was *not* the problem for these couples.

Not only did the partners in these very unhappy marriages communicate perfectly well, they got each other's meaning perfectly well. Men and women do not need translation from the "language" of one sex to that of the other. Especially if they have been partners for a while, they know what the other is trying to convey. When he thinks she's being critical of him, it's because she *is* being critical of him—and they both know it. And when she thinks he's trying to avoid her, hiding down there in the basement with his computer, she's right. He's not just surfing the net. He's in the basement because he doesn't want to be anywhere near *her*. They both know that.

When couples in unhappy marriages do have communication problems, it's generally not because the communication problems caused the marriage problems but the other way around: The marriage problems caused the communication problems. It's easy enough to see why. The emotional tension of being in an unhappy marriage—the disappointment, the resentment, the rage—makes it hard to sit there quietly, listen to your partner attentively, and respond reasonably.

The fundamental problem for many couples in unhappy marriages is not communication but rather understanding. *The partners fail to understand each other,* despite *their ability to communicate. They understand* what *their partners are saying, but they don't understand* how *their partners could say that—how their partners could think and feel as they say they do.*

You may be familiar with that kind of failure in mutual understanding from your own relationships, whether romantic or nonromantic. For example, you may have had the experience of debating a passionately held belief (on abortion or gun control or the like) with someone who held an opposite view. You each understood what the other was saying, but you both walked away from the encounter unable to understand how the other could think and feel as he or she did. You were too different from each other, as people, to understand each other in an *empathic* way. Or, to take a hypothetical, and much more extreme, example, a highly articulate serial killer—think of Hannibal Lecter in *Silence of the Lambs*—could eloquently explain why he does what he does, but you wouldn't be able to connect with the experience behind the words and understand what it might be like to be him. You and he are too different from each other, and words can't bridge that gulf in understanding.

The articulate, unhappily married people who complain of communication problems don't understand each other *as people* because they are so different from each other that even their highly skillful communication can't bridge the gulf in their mutual understanding.

And that's the problem with the idea that communication is the key to happy marriage: It doesn't take into account that, for empathic understanding between people, communication is not enough. For people to be happy in their marriage they must be able to understand not just what their partner is saying, but the experience behind the words. When people are different from each other—when they are not compatible—they cannot do that. They cannot understand what it's like to be their partner—to understand their partner empathically—and the best communication in the world won't help.

Commitment

"Commitment" sounds lofty, and it is high on many therapists' lists of essential ingredients for a good marriage. Frequently used marital-assessment questionnaires inquire into spouses' commitment. And I must confess, I ask almost every couple I see to rate their present level of commitment to their marriage. But, like good communication, strong commitment is more a result of happy marriage than a contributor to it. And I think that's as it should be.

"Commitment," like any word, can be used to mean different things. The dictionary defines "commitment" as "the state of being obligated or emotionally impelled." When I ask people to tell me how committed they are to their marriage, I tell them that all I mean by that is how much they want to stay married.

People can be highly committed to their marriage for a variety of reasons that have nothing to do with happiness. Some people are committed to their marriage because they pledged to stay in it. This comes closest to the dictionary's definition, and there is no arguing with it. If someone wants to stay in a marriage because of a pledge made to spouse or God, then that is what he or she must do. Other people are committed to their marriages because they are financially dependent on their spouse. No matter how unhappy they are in the marriage, they see no way they could survive, economically, outside it. This was the case for many women in my parents' generation, before the economic disparity between men and women started to improve in the 1970s, partly as a result of the women's movement. Some people are committed to staying married because they are dependent on their spouse in some other way—emotionally, for example. Unhappy as they may be, they cannot conceive of living alone. And, of course, many people feel committed to the marriage for the sake of the children.

The point is that commitment coexists with great unhappiness in many marriages. Commitment guarantees nothing about how happy a marriage will be. All it guarantees is that the marriage will continue.

For most of us who do not feel unalterably bound by our marriage vows and who are not dependent on our spouses in some limiting way, how committed we are depends on how happy we are. This makes sense, and it is how we respond in other domains of life. If our job is unrewarding and meaningless, we try to find another job if we can. If the ethnic or religious traditions we were born into come to feel alien or stifling to us, we don't practice them as our parents did, or we don't practice them at all. Why on earth stick with something that is frustrating and makes you unhappy?

And sure enough, in most couples who come in for marital therapy, the commitment of one of the spouses, or both of them, is wavering. Marital therapists ask these couples about their commitment because in marital therapy things often get worse before they get better, if they get better. Highly committed people will be more likely to cooperate with the treatment and to endure the pain that precedes the gain.

Naturally, there is a reciprocal relation between commitment and happiness in marriage. When couples who are not happy let each other know that their commitment is wavering, that itself further increases their unhappiness with the relationship, which leads to even less commitment. When happy spouses let each other know that they want to stay married forever, that increases their sense of security and their happiness, and leads to even more commitment. I have seen lots of couples who are committed because they are happy, but I have never seen a couple who were happy because they were committed.

Hard Work

This one's my favorite. Some writers of self-help books on marriage say two contradictory things without seeming to realize the contradiction. First, they say, "I believe in marriage," by which they mean that they believe that marriage is a good way to achieve happiness. Then they say—and I bet they feel virtuous when they say this—"Marriage is hard work."

When was the last time you went on vacation to do hard work—to the Gulag, perhaps—instead of going to the seashore, or to the mountains, or on a cruise? Hard work is not something that makes people happy. It is something that people avoid if they have the chance. And so a marriage that is hard work is, by definition, not a happy marriage.

Now, maybe all that these writers mean is that marriage takes persistent effort. I can't argue with that because any long-term project takes persistent effort. But if the project makes you happy, you don't experience the effort as hard work. You experience it as fun. For instance, you might spend hours trying to perfect your golf swing or your tennis serve. You might even say, "I work hard at it." But what you mean by that is that you devote persistent effort to it. You experience that effort as fun. Otherwise, you wouldn't do it. If people in unhappy marriages had experienced their courtships as being hard work, as their marriages are, they wouldn't have gotten married.

Happy marriages are not hard work, and happily married people will tell you so. A friend and colleague of mine, Victoria, is in her seventies, is a marital therapist herself, and has been happily married for almost fifty years. When I told her I was writing this book, her first question was "What do you think of the notion that marriage is hard work?" I told her I thought it was baloney and she replied, "I'm so glad you said that."

In a happy marriage, things go relatively smoothly. Most decisions are made with very little conflict. In fact, much of the time there is spontaneous agreement and so there is no need for "communication" or "negotiation":

"I don't feel like cooking tonight. Let's eat out."
"You know, I was thinking the same thing myself."

Or even:

"Dear, I think it's time we had another baby."
"Are you serious?"
"Yes, I'm not kidding. I really mean it."
"OK. Let's go for it."

This may seem too good to be true, especially the second example. As a matter of fact, that is exactly how much "negotiation" it took for a happy couple I know to decide to have their second and third children.

There is disagreement in happy marriages, naturally. And there is conflict, sometimes heated conflict. But conflict is the exception rather than the rule. When it happens, it generally doesn't last long. And while it may sometimes be heated, it is never venomous.

Happy marriage feels easy. It doesn't feel like hard work. Unhappy marriage does feel like hard work because it is. Trying to improve an unhappy marriage is certainly hard work. And as any marital therapist will attest, and as the research on the effectiveness of marital therapy confirms, that hard work often turns out to be fruitless.[2]

But don't despair. Here comes the good news.

2

THE ANSWER:
COMPATIBILITY

THE KEY TO HAVING A HAPPY MARRIAGE IS TO CHOOSE THE RIGHT PER-
SON FOR YOU IN THE FIRST PLACE. THAT PERSON IS SOMEONE WITH
WHOM YOU ARE DEEPLY CÓMPATIBLE—SOMEONE WHO IS VERY SIMILAR
TO YOU ON THREE MAJOR DIMENSIONS: THE PRACTICAL DIMENSION, THE
SEXUAL DIMENSION, AND THE WAVELENGTH DIMENSION.

Why Compatibility?

I have been doing marital therapy for more than twenty years. By the time
I started doing marital therapy, my wife and I had been married for five
years and had gone through, and come out of, the rocky period in our
marriage. By the time I'd been doing marital therapy for ten years, and
been married fifteen, I found myself becoming fatalistic about the couples
who came in for marital therapy. That is, by the end of the second session,
for sure, and often by the end of the first, I had a gut sense that a couple
either had or didn't have what it took (whatever that was) to have a happy
marriage. I hadn't felt like this at the beginning of my career. Back then,

I'd felt that any couple could be helped if only they and I worked hard enough.

I was surprised by my fatalism. After all, I'd learned something about how to do marital therapy over the years, and I had reason to believe that I'd become better at it. Theoretically, that accumulated experience should have made me feel that I could help more couples rather than fewer. But that's not how I felt. As time went on, this fatalistic sense grew stronger that I could help some of the couples I worked with, but that, no matter what, I couldn't help some of the others.

I set about trying to focus in on this vague gut sense to understand what accounted for it. What were the couples doing—what were they showing me—that made me feel either optimistic or pessimistic about them? The first answer that occurred to me was the idea that (for convenience, let's just talk about "good-gut" versus "bad-gut" couples) good-gut couples just liked each other better than the bad-gut couples did. Maybe what these couples were conveying was the sense that underneath all the anger, disappointment, and hurt, they just liked each other as people in a way that the other couples did not. I used this idea as a working hypothesis with the next several couples I worked with—many couples, actually—and I had to admit that my hypothesis was wrong. I was still getting either a good-gut or bad-gut reaction in the first session or two, but it wasn't because some couples liked each other and some couples didn't. In all the couples the level of mutual dislike was high, right up there with the anger, disappointment, and hurt. And I had to admit to myself that this made sense: How can you like someone you're angry at, who you feel has disappointed you and even hurt you? You can't. Something was radiating from those good-gut couples, but not exactly that deep down they liked each other—something else.

Eventually, after being with many more couples, I came up with another handle: *respect*. This felt closer to my gut feeling, and it made more sense, because we *can* respect someone even while we dislike them—even while we feel angry at them. We continue to respect that person because we can't deny that they still have qualities that are valuable and admirable.

What was the source of that mutual respect? Watching yet more couples, I observed that the couples who respected each other had a level of mutual understanding that the couples who didn't respect each other didn't have. In couples with mutual respect, the partners often didn't like what the other had to say *but they got it.* They could understand *why* the other was feeling the way that he or she was: why what was important to the other was important to them—why the other was angry, disappointed, hurt. They respected each other because they were able at least to understand each other's reality.

In the couples without mutual respect, the partners didn't get it. They couldn't understand why the other felt the way that they did; they couldn't understand how *anyone* could feel the way that their partner did. In these couples, the partners talked past each other. And as I watched them talk past each other I saw contempt, impatience, and intolerance in both the speaker and the listener. Each considered the other to be evil, stupid, or crazy. In the bad-gut couples, the partners *couldn't* respect each other because they didn't understand each other—no matter how well they communicated.

Once it is clear that mutual respect is based on mutual understanding, it is easy enough to see what mutual understanding is based on: *similarity*. People who are similar in their values, priorities, tastes, personal habits, opinions, and interests have a much easier time understanding each other, and consequently respecting each other, than people who are very different from each other. If you have a partner who is devoted to football, and you are not, it's hard for you to appreciate exactly what it is he gets out of all those hours he spends in front of the TV; as a result, you might consider your partner a couch potato, or worse. But if you, too, are devoted to football, you're right there in front of the TV with him, and you consider his emotional involvement in the game cute or endearing. You understand that emotional involvement because you feel it yourself. It can't possibly be stupid, or bad, or crazy.

My clinical practice, and I suspect that of most marital therapists, is full of couples who are just too dissimilar to be able to understand and respect each other—too dissimilar to have a happy marriage. Paul and Justine are an extreme example. They were both from a culture where marriages are arranged—even in upper-class Americanized families such as the ones they came from. They were introduced (when she was a college sophomore and he was in his second year of law school) and liked each other well enough at first meeting to want to see each other again. (Arranged marriages are not necessarily shotgun marriages. The families don't choose the specific mate for their child, just the pool of candidates from which their child is allowed to choose. If the child doesn't like one candidate, another one is introduced.) Over the next year and a half, Paul and Justine went out several more times—sporadically, because they were going to school on different coasts. They were getting along well enough, so they finally got married, and their families were satisfied.

By the time Paul and Justine came to see me, they had been married four years and had a three-year-old daughter. It was immediately clear that they were very different people. Although they were both young, Paul was considerably older than Justine. And the contrast between his dark gray business suit and her colorful, casual outfit made the age difference appear even greater, almost as if they were parent and child instead of husband and wife. They also differed in educational attainment and in what is commonly called "intelligence." Justine had never finished college, but Paul had received his law degree and was now working in the patent department of a high-tech company in New Jersey. Justine stayed home with their daughter and intended to remain a homemaker. Paul had more psychometric intelligence, the kind of intelligence that enables people to score high on IQ tests and do well in school. Justine had more emotional intelligence, the kind that enables people to function well in interpersonal situations, and to be optimistic and resilient in the face of adversity.[1]

Neither of these people could fathom what the other was all about. Justine couldn't understand how Paul could spend so much time reading the paper and watching the news on television. Paul couldn't understand how she could spend so much time on the phone with her friends, discussing the characters in soap operas. As Justine complained to me about how impatient Paul was with her, and how she couldn't get him to talk with her about her concerns, I watched Paul seethe with contempt. Paul and Justine were so different in their interests, their concerns, and their outlook on life that they really had nothing to say to each other. Individually they were perfectly interesting as people. They just weren't interesting to each other.

In choosing each other, Paul and Justine did not choose the right person. People have to be much more similar to each other than they were to have a chance at a happy marriage. But similar how, and how much?

The Three Dimensions of Compatibility

Put differently, in what *ways* do people have to be similar to have the mutual understanding and respect that make a happy marriage possible? Thinking about my own marriage, I realized that the partners don't have to be similar about everything, and that they can be dissimilar about some very important things and still be happy. I am an avid and dedicated musician. Music is just about the most important thing in the world to me. My wife is not really interested in music. But we still have a terrific marriage because despite that big difference, we are very close to each other on the three dimensions I mentioned at the start of this chapter: the *Practical Dimension,* the *Sexual Dimension,* and the *Wavelength Dimension.* It's time to explain what each dimension is.

The Practical Dimension

This dimension is called "practical" because it refers to how you manage all the practical decisions of daily life: when to wake up in the morning, what to have for breakfast, how to get the dishes done and the house cleaned, how much money to spend on a car, where to spend your vacation, and how often to visit with your parents. Some of these things are big things—buying a car, for example, or dealing with your parents. Some of them may seem like little things—breakfast, or getting the dishes done—but life is made up of little things. Every day a couple has to make scores of decisions on little, practical issues like these; every year they make thousands. And because the partners have to come to some kind of agreement on each one of these decisions, those "little things" are not truly little. They're all really pretty big.

How any individual person makes these decisions depends on that person's everyday tastes, habits, and preferences. Some people like modern furniture, some like traditional. Some people are morning people, some are night owls. Some people like to eat dinner on a tray in front of the television, some like to eat dinner formally, at the dining room table. Some people like to go out to the movies, some prefer to bring videos in.

Some people like to go to the seashore for vacation, some prefer the mountains.

Each of us has our preferred and habitual way of going about our life day by day, hour by hour, minute by minute—our modus vivendi. The problem is that marriage consists of coordinating two lives, each with its own established modus vivendi. Life goes much more smoothly, day by day, hour by hour, if the modus vivendi of one partner closely matches that of the other.

If the partners do match that way, then most of the time, when a decision comes up, they just spontaneously agree. They both want to have dinner now rather than later, or buy the blue chair rather than the green one.

Partners who are not so closely matched on modus vivendi don't spontaneously agree as often—and so, they have to negotiate. The trouble is that no one is very good at negotiating. And we're all worse at negotiating with our partner than with anyone else in the world. That's because we expect our partner to agree with us in a way we don't expect other people to. If a coworker disagrees with us, we may feel irritated, but we can understand it. It's basically OK for our coworker to disagree with us because we consider that person "someone else." Our partner, though, is not exactly "someone else." We have come to identify with our partner so closely that we think of them as "us," and so we expect them to agree with us because, after all, they're us. So when our partner disagrees with us it's not OK—because we don't expect it and we don't understand it. Our partner is "supposed" to agree with us. When our partner doesn't agree with us, we feel betrayed. That sense of bafflement and betrayal is what makes marital conflict so hot and what makes it such an advantage to just spontaneously agree.

Similarity on the Practical Dimension is important because, to the degree that marital partners are not *similar on it, their day-to-day life together will be harder.*

Just how hard life can get when partners are not close on the Practical Dimension is illustrated by Bill and Donna. When I opened the door to meet Bill and Donna for the first time, I was struck by what a great-looking couple they were. Bill was tall, athletically built, and with chiseled features and wavy dark hair that reminded me of Michelangelo's

David. Donna was almost as tall as Bill and also statuesque, but with radiant blonde hair. Each of them looked great individually, but they looked really great together, summing up, as they did, the ideal of physical perfection. Bill and Donna were both in their early thirties, they had been married for three years, and they had one child, about a year old.

The story they told was this: They had met on a cruise and were instantly attracted to each other. They were both in their late twenties at the time and on the lookout for someone to marry. For each of them, the other seemed to fit the bill exactly, at least in conventional terms: right religion, right educational level, right occupational level, right amount of good looks, et cetera.

Bill and Donna continued to see each other after they returned from the cruise. But since Bill lived in Chicago and Donna lived in St. Louis, their time together was restricted to weekends. Some weekends, Bill would pack a bag and spend the weekend at Donna's house; other weekends, she'd drive up to spend the weekend with him. Those weekends were wonderful. They got along splendidly living together for a weekend at a time. Eventually they got engaged and got married. Once they started living together for more than two days at a time, and trying to establish a common household (and in a space that wasn't his or hers but theirs), it didn't take long for Bill and Donna to discover that, when it came to everyday tastes, habits, and preferences—modus vivendi—he said "tomato" and she said "tomahto" all the way down the line. Nothing was easy. Everything was an argument. Initially, they wrote off their constant struggle over everything as part of getting used to being married and sharing the same "turf." They thought it would get better in time. It didn't. And when, a couple of years into the marriage, they had their baby, she was just another universe of issues they could disagree about—how warmly to dress her, what to feed her, when to pick her up if she was crying, how often to take her to visit her grandparents, and on and on.

At this point you might be asking, "Couldn't they change to become more like each other?" That's a good question. The answer is "Not really." People can and do change a great deal over their life span. They overcome fears and inhibitions and become more confident. They develop their talents and discover and develop other talents they didn't know they had. They get a clearer idea of what's most important to them. But in all this change, they are not changing *away* from who they were before—they are not changing into somebody else—they are changing into being more fully and completely *themselves*. Psychologists have words for this: differentiation (which refers to developing your own individual personality as someone separate from your family) and self-actualization (which refers to identifying your unique strengths and talents and then developing them to the fullest). Whatever the word, the point is that over the life cycle, people gradually realize who they really are and become more purely and more intensely that person.

We change, but our character doesn't change. We remain essentially ourselves. If we started out very neat—never a dirty dish in the sink—we stay that way. If we started out a bit absentminded—never turning out the lights when we leave the room—we stay that way. If we try very hard, then by a combination of awareness and brute force of will, we can learn to behave a little differently. We can learn to turn the lights out and remembering to turn them out may become a bit easier over time, but it will never come naturally to us. That's not who we are.

But our character is more than the collection of our habits. It also includes our personality and outlook. If we started out with a calm temperament, we generally stay that way. If we started out sensitive and anxious by nature, we may learn, with effort, to better manage our anxiety, but the anxiety persists as our natural and automatic reaction. If we started out cynical we stay that way. If we started out hopeful and accepting, we want to stay that way even when disappointments have forced us to have doubts.

What this means for couples, when the partners are very different from each other in some important way, is that they can't change themselves to be enough like their partner. A major difference between Bill and Donna, which caused conflict between them in almost everything they did, was that Donna liked to do things quickly and Bill liked to do things slowly. Neither of them could change their own characteristic pace any more than they could change from being right-handed to being left-handed. And when they tried to change each other—by complaining to each other or lecturing at each other—all that happened was that they each became more set in their ways.

Leaders in the field of marital therapy have come to realize that if couples are incompatible in important ways, they cannot be changed to become more compatible. All that can be done is to help them cope with and tolerate those incompatibilities. These cutting-edge marital therapists now emphasize "acceptance" rather than "change" in their therapy. They try to help couples build bridges across their incompatibilities so that their marriages can be less conflict-ridden.[2] But even with acceptance, those marriages will never run as smoothly, and certainly will never be as happy, as marriages in which the partners are compatible in the first place. These therapists believe, as I do, that incompatibility between partners is *not* something that develops over time as a result of the marriage. When there is incompatibility in a marriage, it has been there from the very beginning, because of the kinds of people the partners are and have always been.

Bill and Donna, individually, were as mentally healthy as they were gorgeous. There was nothing wrong with either of them. They were just wrong for each other. The moral of their story is that if you want day-to-day life in your marriage to run smoothly and to be free from conflict, marry someone close to you on the Practical Dimension. You won't have to expend energy on acceptance and bridge building. You'll have that energy left over for having fun. Instead of feeling that your daily life at home with your partner is hard labor, you'll feel that when you're home you're on vacation.

The Sexual Dimension

People get married partly for sexual reasons, or at least they ought to. Many people will tell you that as you get older and stay married longer, sex inevitably fades. They tell you jokes: "If you put a jelly bean in a jar for every time you do it in the first year you're married, and remove one from the jar every time you do it after the first year, you'll have jelly beans left in the jar by the time you die." If that's what they've lived, too bad for them. There are other people who don't live their sex lives in that depressing way. For example, in a magazine interview, Bette Midler said that something young people don't know about sex is that it gets better as you get older. That's what many happily married couples will tell you.

For these couples sex, over the years, becomes deeper and more powerful, and an increasingly important part of the marital glue. These partners are close to each other on the Sexual Dimension.

When you and your partner are similar to each other on the Sexual Dimension:

—You are as sexually attracted to your partner as your partner is to you.

—You are as interested in sex, and preoccupied with it, as your partner is.

—You are as comfortable with sexuality, and as knowledgeable about it, as your partner is.

—You want to have sex about as frequently as your partner does.

—Your favorite ways of having sex are similar to your partner's. In particular, there are no sexual activities that you love to do but that your partner hates to do, or vice versa.

Similarity on the Sexual Dimension is important because, to the extent that partners are not *close on it, they feel that life is passing them by.*

The Wavelength Dimension

The best way to understand what I mean by the Wavelength Dimension is to ask yourself this question: If my partner were of the same sex as I am, would that person be one of my very best friends?

So, who are our very best friends? They are the people who get it. When we talk to them, we don't have to explain ourselves—they instantly understand. And not only do they understand what we are saying, they *affirm* it. That is, they approve of what we said, and they approve of us for having said it. Likewise, when they talk to us, they don't have to explain themselves to us because we get it. And we not only understand them, we affirm them. When we are with them or even just talking to them on the phone, we have a sense of emotional, intellectual, and spiritual communion; a sense of being "in tune" somehow; of being "on the same wavelength."

To be on the same wavelength is to share the same outlook on life, to see it with the same eyes. When we are on the same wavelength with someone, we have the same attitudes about the big questions in life: about what is important and not important, about what constitutes "the good life," and about what makes life worth living. We agree on what kind of world we see around us and how we would like that world to be different. We share the same spiritual understandings: about how—or even whether—this world and our individual life in it make sense; about God's part in our destiny and that of other people; about why there is suffering and evil in the world; about our ability to control our own destiny; and about what love is and the part love plays in our life.

Speaking of love, here's a story I love to tell that shows how people can get an inkling of whether they're on the same wavelength simply by comparing their reactions to a movie—a movie about love. I call this story "The *Elvira Madigan* Story."

The *Elvira Madigan* Story

Once upon a time, a long time ago (1967, actually), I went out on a date with a beautiful young woman. Let's call her Jennifer. We went to see a Swedish art film of the time called . . . you guessed it. The title character is a young woman in Sweden about a hundred years ago. She is a circus performer who falls passionately in love with a young army officer. He falls passionately in love with her, too. The only problem is—you guessed right again—he's married. The movie is about how beautiful and passionate their love for each other is, with lots of pretty scenes of fields and flowers and music by Mozart constantly playing in the background. Unfortunately for Elvira and her boyfriend, love affairs like theirs were just not tolerated in the Sweden of that time. Sensing that society is closing in on them, and that their love is doomed, Elvira and her boyfriend decide that the only way they can honor and preserve their love is to commit double suicide—which they do with a revolver, in a beautiful field, with Mozart playing. *Bang bang,* they're dead, roll the credits.

Jennifer and I walked out of the movie. She was crying and blowing her nose, talking breathlessly about how beautiful and moving and profound the movie was. I said something like "Oh yeah. It was great."

I *hated* that movie. I thought it was complete baloney, just a load of false sentimentality. As far as I was concerned, it said nothing true—forget about "profound"—about the nature of life or love. Now, at the time, I was only nineteen years old, and like many nineteen-year-old boys, I didn't know a whole lot about relationships. But somehow I had the presence of mind to say to myself, "Sam, if she loved the movie and you hated it, there can't be any future for the two of you, no matter how hot she is. You just see the world too differently. You couldn't possibly ever really understand each other."

Soon afterward the relationship with beautiful Jennifer fizzled out. And a few months later I started going out with another beautiful young woman. I figured I would give her the *Elvira Madigan* test. I asked her, "Did you see *Elvira Madigan?*" She said, "Yeah." I said, "What did you think of it?" She said, "I hated it."

I married her. Not right then and there, of course—some years later. We are still married. And we still share the same outlook. We are still on the same wavelength. And, what is most interesting, as we've grown older, learned more, and as our attitudes on the big questions have evolved and changed, we've remained on the same wavelength. For instance, at the start of our relationship we were both at one point in the political spectrum. But over the years we both have moved to a different point in that spectrum. Each of us moved by a different route, in terms of the experiences and ideas that influenced us, but we arrived at the same point in the end.

This relates to what I said a little earlier about people changing in the direction of becoming more fully themselves. Often couples have said to me, "We grew apart." That's how they felt, certainly, but that's not exactly what happened. What happened was that they *had been* apart from the very beginning, but their own individual identities were not yet developed enough and distinct enough for them to be able to see that. It's as if they are two people standing side by side in a photo that is out of focus, and it looks like they're standing right next to each other with their bodies touching; but then, as the image comes into focus, it becomes clear that they are not touching—there's been a space between them all along.

When people start close to each other on the Wavelength Dimension, they stay close to each other no matter how they change. As a matter of fact, the more they change, the more they realize how close they are. Throughout the lifelong path of change they remain companions.

Similarity on the Wavelength Dimension is important because, to the degree that partners are on the same wavelength, they continue to feel a sense of companionship *with each other. To the degree that they are not on the same wavelength, they feel* lonely *in the relationship.*

There are so many couples where the partners are lonely in the relationship that if I had a nickel for every one of them, I wouldn't have to write this book to get rich. Prince Charles and Princess Diana are one example, maybe the most famous one. The reasons that couples like Charles and Diana are so very different on the Wavelength Dimension seem obvious: differences in age, education, and life experience. But people can match up closely in these ways and still be far apart on the Wavelength Dimension. Richard and Clara are a case in point. They seemed to have a lot in common. They were both very brainy and they both were musicians. They met in their university's orchestra, where he played the violin and she played the cello. He was studying theoretical physics and she was studying economics. They were both very tall, and this was especially important for Clara because she'd always had trouble finding men who were tall enough for her. They were both committed Protestants. When they met, Richard was just coming out of a tempestuous relationship with a woman who he felt was manipulative and overemotional. Richard was attracted by what he saw as Clara's straightforward, uncomplicated, and nonmanipulative nature. For Clara, Richard was very simply the best thing that had ever happened to her: a tall, very intelligent man who was not intimidated by a woman whose intellect was as imposing as her size.

It looked like a good match, but after the marriage Richard and Clara discovered that they were too different on the Wavelength Dimension to affirm each other in some important ways. They found that their political differences were a sore spot. She was politically more conservative than he was. Being as brainy as they were, Richard and Clara were each used to being right in every argument, so they couldn't discuss politics because, with their differing views, they couldn't both be right. They were both religiously committed, but Richard got a lot out of going to church and Clara didn't. And they had huge arguments about Christmas. Clara believed that buying each other expensive presents was how people showed love to each other on Christmas. Richard saw that as going against the religious message of the holiday. Their views on human relations were different, too. Clara's predominant way of viewing people was moral. They were either good or bad, and if they were bad she wanted to have nothing to do with them. As a person who made up theories for a living, Richard tried to devise theories explaining how interacting factors in people's lives caused them to behave as they did. Clara dismissed these as psychobabble. When their daughter was born, their different views about human nature resulted in big fights about the right way to raise her. It was hard for Richard and Clara to feel close when they talked about almost anything important. Eventually they gave up on feeling close. They remained married to each other, but it was a lonely relationship for both of them. And although they did remain faithful to each other sexually, they sought out other people to talk with about the things that were really important to them—people who would understand—so that they wouldn't feel so painfully lonely. It wasn't that Richard and Clara differed in their intellectual and educational levels as, for example, Paul and Justine did. It was just that they didn't see the world in the same way. They were not on the same wavelength.

When people are lonely, as Richard and Clara were, they feel cut off not only from their partner but from *themselves*. It works like this: Each of us has a sense of who we most truly are. When we are young and undifferentiated, we may not be able to put that sense into words, but we have it. As we develop and become more ourselves, we can be more articulate about it. When we and somebody else are on the same wavelength— when each of us understands the other—we feel free to be who we most truly are with that person. And being the person we most truly are is how we are most comfortable and most happy. When we are in a relationship with someone who is not on our wavelength, we do not feel free to be who we most truly are because that person doesn't get it. With someone who is not on the same wavelength, we inhibit ourselves and edit ourselves in many different ways, consciously and unconsciously. We feel like we are in a straitjacket. You may have heard someone say, "I couldn't be myself," or "I lost myself in that relationship." This is what that person was talking about.

When people talk about why their marriages broke up, they talk much more about having been unable to be their true self with their partner than they do about problems with communication and problem solving.[3] And when they do mention communication problems, what they mean is not that they didn't have communication skills. They mean that they and their partner were too different to really understand each other and feel close, no matter how skilled they were at communicating. The best communication skills in the world couldn't have turned me into someone who loved *Elvira Madigan* or Jennifer into someone who hated it.

If you are not on the same wavelength as your partner, then you can't feel like your true self in a large chunk of your life, and you start to miss that feeling. What happens to many people in this predicament is that they discover they can be their most true self in some other domain of their life—in their job, for example. Say that Tony and Tamara each feel cut off from their own most true self in their marriage because they are not on the same wavelength. Tony feels he can be his most true self at his job as a creative person in an advertising agency. As a result, he starts to feel more connected to his job than to Tamara. Tamara notices this and complains that Tony is more in love with the job than he is with her. She's right. If Tony discovers that he is on the same wavelength as Terri, who works in his office, he'll find himself being able to feel like the true Tony when he's with her. And he may find himself falling in love with her.

Prince Charles was quoted as saying that he never really loved Diana. Clearly there is some connection between similarity on the Wavelength Dimension—and on the other two compatibility dimensions—and what might be called lasting love. It's time to see how love fits in.

3

HOW LOVE FITS IN

Let's start with romantic love, since that always comes before lasting love and forms part of the basis for it—that is, in those couples for whom romantic love does evolve into lasting love. I propose this definition:

Romantic love is the special excitement you feel when you realize that someone you are physically attracted to is attracted to you.

This one sentence does not describe the experience of romantic love in its totality, but it does put its finger on the switch that kicks the entire mechanism of romantic love into action. If you have any doubts that physical attraction is at the center of romantic love, do this thought experiment. (Maybe you don't have to do this as a thought experiment; maybe it's happened to you.) Imagine finding out that someone you consider physically unattractive is attracted to you and would like to go out with you. Does that send romantic tingles through you or does it give you the creeps? So, let's agree for now that physical, sexual attraction is the mainspring of romantic love. It's what gets romantic love going and it's what powers it.

Most authors of popular books on relationships and marriage disparage romantic love. They dismiss romantic love as an illusion, as counterfeit, as deception and self-deception. They place it as opposite to "true love," which they regard as real, genuine, and honest. They are wrong. Romantic love is just as real as "true love" (which I'll continue to term "lasting love"). It is just as genuine, in the sense of being justified and sincere. And although there is a willful element to romantic love, it is not some kind of trick we play on ourselves or on each other. The processes that go on between two people in romantic love, and inside each of their heads, are largely the same as those of lasting love. Lasting love is not the opposite of romantic love, it's the extension of romantic love. The only important difference between romantic love and lasting love is that the fuel supply for romantic love is limited, so eventually it stops, while the fuel supply for lasting love is unlimited.

LET'S START by taking a closer look at what happens in romantic love. You and someone physically attractive to you let each other know that you are attracted to each other. What is being exchanged right there, at the very start? *Approval.* Each of you receives the information that the other approves of something very important to you, something crucial to your sense of who you are and to your self-esteem: your looks. It is in this sense that romantic love is real and genuine. Given the obvious importance to each of us of our physical/sexual nature, what better reason is there to begin to fall in love than for the reason that someone is attracted to us in that way? The message that this attractive person approves of your looks is powerful for many reasons—because it is reassuring, because it boosts your confidence, but most of all because it suggests that this attractive person might want to have sex with you sometime.

You spend time together, you get to know each other a bit—maybe you even sample each other sexually—and you both like what you're discovering about each other. You allow yourself to begin to "fall" into romantic love.[1] You continue to give each other messages that you approve of that very important aspect of the other—the physical/sexual aspect. And as you get to know other aspects of this new person, you show approval of those aspects too. You very much want to approve of other aspects of this physically attractive person because you want them to stick around—and you know how important their overall approval is to you. During this process of getting to know each other, each of you is naturally on your best behavior. Some writers on romantic love charge that there's something deceitful about that, but they are wrong. There's nothing dishonest about being the best you can be with someone you're falling in love with. The most admirable things about you as a person are really you—otherwise you wouldn't be able to display them to someone else. The part of you that enables you to write romantic love notes is no less real a part of you than the part that allows you to quietly pick your nose, just a little, now and then, when nobody's looking.

It's easy to find lots to approve of about each other, motivated as you are by romantic love. And since you are just getting to know each other, there is something new to approve of, and to be approved for, every day. This is what gives romantic love its excitement. Mutual approval—or to use a slightly fancier word from chapter 2, affirmation—is what romantic love is all about.

This process of mutual affirmation leads directly to the sense of mutual caring in romantic love. It is this sense, that the other is there for you and you are there for the other, which gives you the feeling that this is really love and not just infatuation. You are each grateful for the other's affirmation of you, and that gratitude disposes you to feel kind and generous toward each other. You come to feel that the other's happiness and well-being are as important to you as your own, and you act accordingly. If the other is hurt or upset, you try to soothe them. If the other is reaching for some goal, you try to give them a boost. At the very least, you root for them. Each of you is confident that the other is on your side, ready to back you in any way they can. Whatever the challenge you're facing, you're not facing it completely alone.

There is more to romantic love, as we all know, than mutual affection and caring. There is the blissful preoccupation that each of you has with the other, the elaborate daydreams you spin about your future together, and the sense of being completed in some way by the other. But mutual affirmation and caring are at the center of romantic love, *just as they are at the center of lasting love*. Romantic love and lasting love don't differ on that score. They differ only with respect to fuel supply.

The huge affirmation machine that is romantic love is powered by sexual energy. Inevitably, that sexual energy diminishes. As you get to know each other better sexually, your sexual curiosity about each other becomes satisfied, and you become somewhat habituated to each other as a sexual stimulus. Your naked bodies come to be associated not just with sex but with a variety of other activities, including, occasionally, arguing. Not only that—you begin to take it for granted that this other person is physically attracted to you. You become habituated to that, too.

The sexual energy in your relationship doesn't go down to zero—far from it—but it does go down enough so that it can no longer power the automatic mutual affirmation of each other's nonsexual self in the way it did at the start. What's more, as time passes, there is less to find out about each other. And even if there were a steady stream of new things to find out about the other, you wouldn't view them as positively as you had at the start because that superintense level of sexual energy between you isn't there anymore.

Once your relationship reaches that point, you will have enough mutual affirmation to maintain continued, lasting love only if you are close enough to each other on the three dimensions of compatibility— starting with the Sexual Dimension. At the start, when the sexual novelty is high, it's easy to feel as if you and your partner are close on the Sexual Dimension. Once that novelty tapers off, you and your partner will be able to find out if, in fact, you *are* close on it. If you are, your sexual relationship will continue to grow and deepen. If you're not close on the Sexual Dimension, you will find yourself a lot less interested in sex with your partner than you had been, and wondering why.

And once the superabundant sexual energy of romantic love has dissipated a bit, you will be able to find out if you two are actually close enough on the other two dimensions so that you can continue to affirm each other and maintain lasting love. Think about the Practical Dimension. If both of you like to go out to a loud club and dance on Saturday night, then you can affirm each other by doing that; or if you both prefer to sit home and watch videos, you can affirm each other by doing that. But if one of you prefers to go to a club and the other prefers old movies, the two of you will have to come up with some other way to affirm each other on Saturday night. If you both like to roam flea markets looking for antiques, you can affirm each other doing that, but if one of you thinks that antiques are old, moldy junk, you can't. If you both like to occasionally do something impulsive and extravagant like splurging at a fancy restaurant, you can both do that and affirm each other, or if both of you like searching out cheap but good little places to eat, you can both do that and affirm each other. But if one of you thinks that spending a week's grocery money on dinner for two, even once in a while, is wasteful, or if one of you finds cheap little restaurants depressing, you can't do either. You'd both end up feeling irritated instead of affirmed.

Now look at the Wavelength Dimension. If becoming a millionaire is a major life goal for both of you, you will affirm each other as you strive for that. If serving mankind in some way is how you both want to live your life, you will affirm each other as you go about trying to do that. But if one of you wants to be Bill Gates and the other wants to be Mother Teresa, then you two will regard each other either as coldhearted or as a sap. Likewise, if one of you considers your shared religious heritage to be enriching and meaningful and the other considers it outdated superstition, it will be hard for either of you to feel that the other approves of your views about humankind's place in the universe. If one of you is a liberal, left-wing Democrat and the other is a radical, right-wing Republican, and if you talk with each other about politics at all, you will argue. And the arguments will be painful because you will feel that your partner disapproves not only of your political views but of *you*. If, on the other hand, your political positions coincide, you'll be able to feel righteous together.

The more alike you and your partner are on the two nonsexual dimensions, there will be not only more mutual affirmation, but also a stronger sense of mutual caring. If the two of you are very different, a sense of mutual caring will be harder to come by. If you approve of what your partner thinks or wants to do, you will be supportive. If, for instance, you both want to become millionaires, and your partner is engaged in a desperate battle for control inside their corporation, you will want to give your partner as much aid and comfort as you can. It will be harder for you to do that if you consider your partner's career aspirations to be unworthy.

Roland and Francine experience the mutual caring that comes from being on the same wavelength. They met in college and it didn't take them long to discover that they both passionately wanted to get rich. That didn't take them long either. They attended the same prestigious business school together, and after graduation they moved to the part of the country that looked most promising to them and got jobs at fast-growing companies. At every step along the way Roland and Francine supported each other and helped each other: in studying for tests and writing papers, preparing for interviews, evaluating business opportunities, and dealing with corporate politics. Each rejoiced at the other's sucesses and helped the other recover from setbacks. As Francine put it, "I'm Roland's trainer and manager, and he's mine."

Once you and your partner have gotten past the stage of romantic love, the affirmation and caring between you—love, in short—can continue only if you have the mutual understanding and respect that come from being similar enough to each other—that is, compatible.

One more thing: The more alike you are, especially on the Wavelength Dimension, the more interesting you'll continue to find each other. You might think it would be the other way around—the more different, the more interesting—but it isn't. Think of it like this: Suppose you go to a movie with a coworker who is not a particularly good friend of yours. After the movie you are not particularly interested in what your coworker has to say about it, because you each reacted very differently to it. You two can't connect on the movie. You don't have enough in common, in the way you each understood the movie, to sustain a conversation. So you have a quick coffee and you go your separate ways. Now, suppose you go to the movie with one of your very best friends. You're very interested in what your friend has to say about the movie because their reaction to it is close enough to yours so that you can really understand each other. In fact, you understand each other's reaction to the movie so well that, in your conversation, each of you helps the other better understand *their own* reaction. And that is what an interesting conversation is all about.

If your partner is one of your very best friends—if you're that much alike on the Wavelength Dimension—then you stay interested in each other because you two are interested in the world in the same way; and this ever-changing world we live in gives the two of you infinite raw material for staying interested in it together, and for staying interested in each other. You never get bored with each other.

When you and your partner are close on the Practical Dimension, *and* on the Sexual Dimension, *and* on the Wavelength Dimension—when your love is *three-dimensional*—it can last for a very long time.

Partners who are not compatible on these dimensions sooner or later find themselves falling out of love with each other. That's what happened to Jane, the person described on the first page of chapter 1, who was mystified by why she didn't love her husband anymore. As she told her story it wasn't a mystery to me, and it won't be a mystery to you now that you've read this far into the book: Jane had met Bob toward the end of college and he was, as she put it, "perfect." He was intelligent, handsome, kind, polite, and career-oriented. To top it off, he liked her too. Everyone said they made a great couple. After going out for a few years, getting married seemed inevitable, especially considering they'd been involved for so long. But even before the wedding Jane had qualms, which she tried her best to ignore. It didn't take long after the wedding for Jane to realize that she should have taken her qualms seriously. Even before the marriage, Jane had wondered about why the sexual bond between her and Bob had weakened. She'd been puzzled too about why, so often, they didn't seem to have a whole lot to say to each other. And although Bob was polite and kind, he'd always been a bit critical of her. He was critical gently, but he was critical. He would comment that her behavior was not as refined as he might have liked: the way she held her knife and fork, some of the words and phrases she used when she spoke. Bob was a devoted triathlete and spent a huge number of hours training; Jane loved golf. Bob was a good golfer too, but he didn't have the time for golf with her because of his training schedule. Jane had a great time with the other executives and creative people at her advertising agency; Bob, a dentist, found them irritating.

As I listened to Jane's story, I kept on thinking, "If there's any mutual affirmation going on in this relationship, she hasn't told me about it yet." She never did. There wasn't any.

By the end of the session, after Jane had told me her story, she'd calmed down quite a bit and had stopped crying. Then I said, "Seems like you've been lonely in your relationship with Bob," and she burst into tears once more. She said that, yes, she had felt lonely, very lonely, and that the loneliness had set in even before she and Bob got married.

A few months after her initial interview with me, Jane told Bob that she was leaving him. His first response was to cry. But a few minutes later he told her that he had been making plans to leave her. He'd been lonely, too.

Jane and Bob had both married the wrong person. It was clear that they were not nearly close enough on any of the three dimensions. Jane had sensed at least some of this even before she and Bob got married. Maybe he had sensed it, too. Why, then, did they marry each other? Why do so many people end up marrying someone they're not compatible with? Why do they marry the wrong person?

The standard self-help-book answer is that they are duped by romantic love. That answer is wrong—for two reasons. First, romantic love is true, not false; the problem is just that it doesn't last long enough for the lifetime vows that people make when they get married. Second, love isn't the reason that people get married anyway. People get married because of the pressure to get married. This may sound strange to you now, but it won't once you understand some things about the social, public nature of marriage. Once you understand those things, you'll have a better understanding of why people end up marrying the wrong person.

4

LOVE IS PRIVATE,
MARRIAGE IS PUBLIC

Most people, when they make love, make sure that nobody is watching. When people get married, somebody is always watching—there has to be a witness—and usually *everybody* is watching. Love is private but marriage is public.

The most important thing to understand about marriage is that it's not an interpersonal relationship. It's a legal relationship, as anyone who has ever gotten divorced knows only too well. (You need a license from the state to get married, just as you need one to drive a car, although you have to demonstrate that you know something about driving before you get a driver's license.) You can think of marriage as a sort of legal *container* for the infinite variety of interpersonal relationships that can be poured into it—both good ones and bad.

It's not only the government that is looking over your shoulder as you get married. Your religious denomination is looking, too. Even if you have a state license, you won't be properly married in the eyes of your religion unless you do it according to its rules and regulations.

Why does the whole world act like it has a stake in your getting married? What is all the fuss about?

Marriage and Society

Marriage exists in all societies on Earth. And it has existed in human societies as far back as we can see. Marriage arose as a way to control human reproduction and make it orderly: a way to make clear who was responsible for the care of each new child that came along, and who gained the benefits that came from that child. (We tend to think of children as an expense item, but for most of history children were regarded as an economic asset. They could start to work at a young age and help support the family. And later they would support their parents when the parents got too old to support themselves. In many cultures around the world, children are still thought of in this way.)

In all societies, from the very beginning, marriage has determined not only who is related to each new child who arrives, but how everybody in the group is related to everybody else. It is the elementary form of kinship, determining who is in your close family, your clan, your tribe—and so it is the basic building block of political relations. Marriage also determines property relations: who gets what from whom, and who inherits what from whom. Adjacent lands, or even countries, can become one territory if the owners or the children of the owners marry. And in traditional societies—in Europe until not too long ago, and to this day in many other parts of the world—every marriage included an economic deal: the dowry.

Because marriage is at the center of the social order in these three important ways—reproduction, politics, and economics—it is useful to society that as many people as possible get married and stay married. Marriage is so important to an orderly society that it generally has not been left to chance. It has been arranged. It still is, in some places.

In our society, most marriages are not arranged. Instead of getting paired up by our parents, we get paired up by romantic love. But we're not exactly as free about getting married—especially about whether to get married—as we think we are.

The Pressure to Get Married

After countless generations at the center of human existence, marriage is more than just a matter of law. It is a social *convention*. That is, it is an accepted custom—something that everyone (or almost everyone) agrees is the right and proper thing for people to do. Sometimes we put people down by saying, "Oh, they're so conventional," but there's nothing wrong with acting conventionally. In many situations, life is more pleasant when everyone does act conventionally. We're reminded of that whenever someone breaks a social convention that most of us agree on, such as when someone cuts ahead of us in line.

Most of us agree that getting married sometime in early adulthood is the right and proper thing to do. This is what we have been taught to believe from earliest childhood by the culture we've grown up in. (It is useful, to that culture, that we believe it because if we do we're more likely to get married—and marriage keeps society orderly.) We have also been taught that getting married *means a lot about who we are*. It means, most of all, that we (not just our children) are *legitimate*—that we fit in with the rest of society the way we're supposed to. By getting married we establish ourselves as part of the adult world. As a couple, we become a known quantity to the people in our social environment in a way that is reassuring to them. Getting married means that we have succeeded (and that our parents have succeeded). We have achieved an important life goal, and we are now positioned to achieve other important life goals, such as having children and establishing a home. Finally, if we are religious—no matter what the religion—getting married means that we're fulfilling God's plan for us.

We expect to get married. Our parents, brothers, sisters, and friends expect us to get married. Sooner or later in early adulthood, we begin to experience that shared expectation as *the pressure to get married*. Because women have to be mindful of having children before it's too late, they experience the pressure earlier than men. And women generally feel the pressure to get married more strongly than men. That's because the cultural message that you have to be married to really be somebody has always been beamed more strongly at women. (Have you ever seen a *groom's* magazine?) But men feel the pressure too. Marriage is too important to anyone's image and status for men *not* to feel it.

Women feel the pressure to get married. Men feel the pressure to get married. And so, sometime in early adulthood, we start to be on the lookout for someone not just to have fun with and feel romantic with, but for someone to marry.

Optimizing Versus Satisficing

Whenever the pressure to get married starts for us, once it's on it's really on: We feel a sense of urgency about finding someone to marry. And at the same time we have the sense that our choices are limited. There are the people we see at work, in our classes at school, and the friends of our friends. That doesn't seem like many people. And if we don't feel that confident about our own attractiveness, then we may feel that our choices are even more limited. We figure that we can't afford to hold out for the person who might be ideal for us, or even close, because that person might never cross our path. We figure that if someone in the acceptable ballpark comes along, we ought to make the best of that, even though they may be pretty far from our ideal partner in some important ways. In short, *the pressure to get married causes us to use what psychologists call a "satisficing" decision-making strategy in choosing a partner, instead of the "optimizing" strategy that we use in making other important decisions.*

To get a sense of how different these two strategies are, imagine how you and your partner would go about buying a diamond engagement ring. You wouldn't just buy the first nice-enough ring you saw that was in your price range. (If you *did* do that, you would have been satisficing.) Instead, you would go to several different stores and compare what they had. After seeing a few rings you might realize that there was a certain shape of stone that you preferred, or one kind of setting that you liked more than the others. You might even go so far as to read up a little on diamonds to be sure that you were getting the very best quality in your price range. Only then would you plunk your money down for the ring. You would optimize.

We don't usually optimize like this in choosing a marriage partner. What generally happens is this: We're on the lookout for someone to marry, and so is someone else. We meet that someone else and each of us finds the other physically attractive—attractive enough to become interested in each other. And then we each find out that a) this other person is a nice person, and that b) they're physically attracted to us. This is all we need for the sexually powered process of mutual affirmation to begin: We fall into romantic love. Once we're in romantic love, our partner *looks* right for us in just about every way. And if, as the relationship develops, we continue to find that our partner is a nice person, and we continue to be sexually attracted, we start to think that maybe this one could be The One. And finally, if our partner's demographic characteristics—age, education, occupation, religion, et cetera—are in the acceptable ballpark (as far as we *and* our family and friends are concerned; remember, marriage is public), we can move on to getting engaged and married. Bill and Donna, the "tomato/tomahto" couple in chapter 2, got married in just this way. The many couples who get married the way Bill and Donna did are not optimizing, they are satisficing. They are not selecting the best from a set of alternatives; they are simply deciding that the one alternative they have in front of them is good enough to be the one to choose. The important thing to notice is this: *Although the partners are satisficing, the feeling of romantic love makes them* feel *like they are optimizing—so they feel confident in their decision.*

When people marry as a result of satisficing, everyone is happy at the start. The partners are happy. And their families and friends are happy because, to all appearances, the two of them seem well suited to each other. The partners find out just how well suited to each other they actually are only when the sexual fuel for romantic love has run out—whether that's three days after the wedding, three months, or three years. (It won't take longer than three years.) At that point, if they're lucky, the partners discover that they happened to marry someone who was not only conventionally similar to them, but also similar enough on the Three Dimensions of Compatibility so that they have a lifetime fuel supply for mutual affirmation and lasting love. If they're not lucky, they find that they don't love each other the way they did at the beginning. They may be aware that the love disappeared because they weren't compatible enough. Or they may not be aware of that, and just scratch their heads in disappointment and perplexity.

These unlucky couples would have been better off if they hadn't married each other. And they might not have if it weren't for the pressure to get married. Their romance would have run its course and they would have broken up without the legal problems, stigma, and heartbreak (especially if there already are children) that result from a failed marriage.

At this point you might be objecting to what I've said about optimizing versus satisficing. After all, as a practical matter people can't compare a number of potential mates as they would engagement rings. When we're involved with someone, there usually aren't a bunch of other people hanging around for comparison shopping. And even if there were we wouldn't want to, simply because we're in love with the person we're with. Occasionally people do find themselves in love with two people at the same time, and try to decide between them. The experience of a person in that position is not that of a coolheaded, optimizing decision maker. It is agony—because love is involved.

But optimizing is not simply a matter of being able to choose among several alternatives. It is a matter of having a clear sense of what you're looking for. (Think back to the wedding ring example, in which you decided which setting you liked most, and you intentionally found out what made one diamond different and better than another before you made your choice.) Most people lack a clear sense of what's important to look for in a marriage partner. Often they simply compare their current relationship with previous ones and point to the ways that this relationship is better. But if those previous relationships were really bad in those ways, then the fact that this relationship is better doesn't say much. All it says is that this relationship may be less bad—"good enough." That's the problem with satisficing: When it comes to choosing whom you're going to marry, "good enough" isn't good enough.

The way to optimize your decision about whom to marry is to have a clear sense of how you and your partner compare on each of the dimensions of compatibility. Similarity on these dimensions is what's important to look for. If you make your choice according to how similar you are on these dimensions, you are optimizing and not just satisficing.

You *do not* have to find your clone to be optimizing. You're optimizing as long as you choose someone who is close enough to you on the compatibility dimensions so that you two will have the unlimited fuel supply you need for lifelong mutual affirmation and lasting love. There's a world of difference between someone who is "good enough" for you in the negative sense that they're better than the competition and someone who is truly good enough in the positive sense that they're compatible with you.

But to optimize, you have to be aware of the pressure on you to get married and be able to resist it. Otherwise, you could have big problems.

Bad Vibes, or "Let's Get Married Anyway"

People who use a satisficing strategy and end up with an incompatible partner sometimes find that their romantic love begins to drain away even before the wedding date. That's disappointing and puzzling, of course. But worse, they find that their relationship becomes increasingly governed by their incompatibilities. They find themselves arguing, being irritated with each other, and being troubled by aspects of the other's character that they'd hardly noticed at the beginning. Each feels less affirmed by the other, and they start to feel worried about what their future together will be like. They develop a sense of foreboding: bad vibes.

If the partners listen to their bad vibes and take them seriously, they break up, just as they broke up earlier relationships when the romantic love had run its course and the incompatibilities took over. They break off the engagement and cancel the wedding. But in many cases, couples who have bad vibes about getting married are also feeling the pressure to get married just as strongly—maybe more strongly. They think of all the time they have invested in the relationship, of the risks of starting over—how hard it will be to find someone else and how long it will take to get to this point again. So they go ahead and get married despite their bad vibes.

They try to block out their bad vibes through rationalization: "He'll change his mind about having a child once he's older and more mature." "Her drinking will quiet down once we're married and she's not living alone." "He'll be more responsible about his job once he feels he's settled and making a home." People are enormously creative in coming up with rationalizations. And, of course, there's that old standby, "Marriage is hard work," as in "She's totally irresponsible with her credit cards. Marriage is hard work," or "He hit me again. Marriage is hard work."

Another reason people get married despite their bad vibes is con-fusion—confusion of a very special kind: They confuse attachment with love. They think that what is really just attachment is actually love.

Human beings, like chimps, dogs, and other higher animals who live in social groups, form attachment bonds with those they are close to. When you are attached to someone, you feel that having them around is important for your welfare. And if you become separated from them you will react with grief. The grief reaction always includes sadness, but it can also include fear and even panic. Ordinarily, individuals become attached to the people with whom they have positive, affectionate relationships: their parents, brothers and sisters, and lovers. They become equally attached to the people with whom they have negative, hostile relation-ships: their parents, brothers and sisters, and lovers. Prisoners can become attached to their jailers, and hostages to their captors. The key to becoming attached is not how positive the relationship is, but how closely involved and intense it is.

It is terribly confusing to feel attached to someone with whom you have a negative relationship. It is especially confusing, and troubling, to feel attached to someone with whom you are now in a negative relation-ship but whom you used to love. People who have fallen out of romantic love with their partner, and who are having bad vibes, feel this confusion. They think that their continued feeling of attachment to their partner means they must still love their partner somehow, even though the rela-tionship doesn't seem right in the way it once did.

Elaine was confused like this. Elaine met Gary a few years after her beloved sister had been killed by a drunk driver. In those intervening years, Elaine had been depressed and isolated, so when Gary came into her life he really brightened up her world. Gary also helped Elaine in a variety of practical ways that made her feel cared for. Initially the rela-tionship was great, and Elaine felt real love for him. But as the relation-ship continued, Elaine began to sense a certain spookiness about Gary. He wanted to control Elaine in the most minute ways: how much time she spent seeing her friends, what TV programs she watched, how she dressed, how she made up her face, even what she ate. And although Gary did take care of her in a variety of ways, they were the ways *he* wanted. By the time Gary gave Elaine an engagement ring (the ring *he* wanted), Elaine had stopped loving him: She didn't like him as a person and she'd become turned off to him sexually. But because Elaine was still attached to Gary, she thought that she still did love him. It took a lot of psychotherapy to help her see her confusion and break up with Gary before they got married. Elaine felt terribly sad when she broke up with Gary—there always is grief when an attachment is broken, no matter how bad the relationship—but she gritted her teeth and got through it because she realized she couldn't stay with him.

Sometimes people get married despite bad vibes, not because they are rationalizing or confusing attachment with love, but purely out of the pressure to get married, which they experience as embarrassment, or guilt, or both. For example, when couples get married because of an accidental pregnancy, they are often doing it out of some combination of embarrassment and guilt.

Here's an embarrassment story: As a marital therapist I try my hardest to be neutral in my stance toward the two partners. I try to find something to like about each of them. But with some couples I fail: I just can't help but think that one of them is the villain. Nancy and Karl were such a couple. Nancy was sweet, pretty, and insightful. Karl, on the other hand, was nasty, ugly, and psychologically dense. In his dealings with Nancy he was unreasonable, immature, coercive, and hurtful—one of the meanest people I've ever been faced with in marital therapy.

I don't know what first attracted these very different people to each other. It's long enough ago so that I don't remember, and my notes don't say. Anyway, they did become attracted, involved, and finally, engaged. Sometime after they'd become engaged, Nancy came to the realization that marrying Karl would be a disaster, as indeed it turned out to be. But she went through with it anyway. Why? Because the invitations had already been mailed, and it would have been embarrassing to cancel the wedding.

Here's a guilt story: I met my buddy Mickey in college. Mickey was rich and he always managed to find girlfriends who were rich. A few years after he graduated college he became engaged to one of them: the daughter of a corporate CEO. Mickey was twenty-five at the time, and his fiancée, Rochelle, was twenty-eight.

Eventually, I met Rochelle, and I didn't like her. (Mickey later told me that nobody had liked her—not his parents, not his sisters, nobody.) I was alarmed that Mickey was getting set to marry her and I figured I ought to have some kind of talk with him. I happened to be visiting in New York City, where, as part of his otherwise charmed life, Mickey was working as a record producer. We were walking down West Fifty-seventh Street, talking about his upcoming marriage. It was obvious from the way Mickey was talking that he had some misgivings about marrying Rochelle. I saw my opening and I made my move. I said, "Mickey, why are you marrying her?" Mickey said, and these were his very words, "Well, we've been going together a year and a half, Rochelle's twenty-eight and she wants to get married, and there is nowhere else for the relationship to go—*and if it doesn't work out we can always get divorced.*" My heart sank. You can more or less guess the rest of the story. After several years of a marriage that can only be described as warlike, and children who were caught in the crossfire Mickey and Rochelle did get divorced. (Ultimately the story had a happy ending. Within a few years Mickey married another rich woman, a banker, and that marriage turned out to be happy.)

There is a moral to these stories, and I'm going to state it very emphatically, as a rule, because I believe it so strongly.

The Bad Vibes Rule
Listen to your bad vibes and take them seriously. If you have any doubts, hesitations, or second thoughts, then at least postpone the wedding. If it's become clear to you that entering into this marriage is a mistake, cancel the wedding—and don't let anything or anyone stop you.

Is Optimizing Too Idealistic?

Now that you've read what I think about optimizing versus satisficing, you might well be skeptical. You may be saying to yourself, "That's easy for *him* to say. He lucked out and married a woman he's very compatible with. But what about me? If I had to find someone that perfect in order to be happily married, it would take forever. And anyway, if my partner is a good and decent person, and if I am too, we'll be OK even if we're not very compatible."

I appreciate this point of view. Indeed, we have no guarantee that we ever will meet someone who is really right for us. And if we haven't met that person yet, it's easy to believe that satisficing is the only realistic way to find someone to marry.

In response, let me make two points:

First, I want to reiterate—and I can't say this strongly enough: *You and your partner don't have to be clones of each other to be compatible. You just have to be similar in enough key ways so that there's enough continuing mutual affirmation for you to continue to feel in love.* You can be very different from each other in lots of ways, even in some very important ways, and still be compatible enough to have endless fuel for mutual affirmation. I am not talking about perfection and you shouldn't be looking for it. That's not what optimizing means.

Second, while it's true that you can spend a lot of time looking for the right person—that you can "waste a lot of time being too picky"—it's also true that you can waste a lot of time *not being picky enough*. Let me tell you the story of Sal.

Sal was about forty when I met him. He was a successful, high-level salesman. He was a handsome man and, as far as I could tell, a good-hearted man. Sal had never been married. He wanted to be married and to have children. His problem was that none of his relationships ever lasted more than a year and a half before he wanted out. When Sal came to see me, he was reaching the eighteen-month mark in his relationship with Linda, and sure enough he wanted out. Sal was puzzled by his tendency to quit relationships, and he wanted to understand it.

Now, the standard explanation for this pattern of behavior in a man is that he's "afraid of commitment." But fear of commitment was not Sal's problem. His problem was that he wasn't picky enough. Sal had never developed a very clear idea of what kind of woman would be the right person for him as a long-term partner. He would meet an attractive woman, which was easy for him to do since he was attractive and sweet. He'd start going out with her, they would have a great time together, and soon enough he'd become seriously involved with her. The relationship would be great for a while, but sooner or later Sal would find himself getting bored. He'd find that he really didn't have much to say to her. Chances are that at least some of the women who were involved with Sal found themselves being bored, too.

Sal had many good qualities, and the women he became involved with had many good qualities too, but partners can have many good qualities and still not have the right *combination* of qualities to be compatible. Sal didn't know what that right combination of qualities was for him; and, as it happened, he did not luck out, as people sometimes do, and just stumble across the right person. Each time, the relationship would last much longer than it should have, until Sal finally reached his limit. But meanwhile, eighteen months *had* passed, eighteen months that Sal could have spent looking for a woman who was really right for him, and very possibly finding one—if only he'd had a better idea of what kind of woman that was.

You owe it to yourself to be picky. Spend some time being picky and trying to optimize. Better to "waste" time that way than the way Sal did. You may just find the right person. At the very least, use this book to form a clear idea of who would be the right kind of person for you. That way, you won't be drifting rudderless on the sea of romantic relationships, as Sal did for so many years.

BUT LET'S NOT be overly idealistic. Not everyone gets the chance to marry someone they're really compatible with on all three dimensions. If you think that you may have to satisfice, what you *can* do to increase your chances of happiness is learn what to expect, and what not to expect, out of the different kinds of marriages that result when partners are not compatible on all three dimensions. The next chapter is about those different kinds of marriages. The good news is that some of them can be quite workable.

5

DIFFERENT KINDS
OF MARRIAGES

When people satisfice in choosing their marriage partner, as they mostly do, the kind of partner they end up with is largely a matter of chance. The lucky ones end up with a partner who is close to them on all three compatibility dimensions, someone as well matched to them as they would have chosen if they had optimized. This does happen. After all, some people win the lottery, and some even win it twice.

Most people are not that lucky. They end up with someone they are compatible with on two of the three dimensions, or on only one, or even on none. The different kinds of marriages that result from people being mismatched one way or the other vary in their workability and in their potential for happiness.

Of course, people can be *more or less* similar on any of the dimensions. But there is some critical, threshold point where if the partners are *that* similar they think of themselves as compatible, and if they are not that similar they think of themselves as not compatible. Once partners are compatible, they may be just compatible, or quite compatible, or very compatible. It's analogous to the threshold for hearing: As the loudness of a sound is gradually increased, it gets to a point where we can just begin to hear it, however faintly. Once we can hear the sound, it can become louder and louder; but below that threshold we can't hear it.

In the rest of this chapter, for simplicity's sake, I'll be talking about whether the partners are compatible or not on each of the three dimensions, without making fine distinctions about how compatible they are.

Zero-Dimensional Marriages

If the partners are not compatible on any of the three dimensions, there is no way their marriage can be workable, much less happy. People often enter these marriages impulsively, and for a variety of bad reasons: They are trying to escape from their parents' house; they are on the rebound from a previous relationship; they got pregnant; they're crazy. I'm not kidding about that last one. Howard, for example, married Florence while he was in a manic state. He was not quite psychotic when he married her, but his reasoning and judgment were severely impaired by his mania. Florence was extremely Bad News, which Howard realized as soon as he came down from his manic state. With his reasoning and judgment restored, Howard couldn't imagine how he could have thought it was a good idea to marry Florence, and he immediately left her. And that's what happens more often than not in Zero-Dimensional Marriages: They break up in a matter of months or even weeks.

One-Dimensional Marriages

Marriages where the partners are compatible on only one of the three dimensions are barely workable. They generally don't last, although they don't self-destruct as quickly as Zero-Dimensional marriages. If they do last, they are not happy.

Sex-Only

This is probably the most common One-Dimensional marriage. Sex-Only marriages are generally entered into impulsively and they last only as long as the sex is good. But conflicts between the partners about how to manage their daily life together, and the feeling of not being on the same wavelength, cause the sex to go sour sooner than it would have if the partners had stayed single, spared each other the torture of living together, and limited the relationship strictly to sex.

Phyllis and Wayne met at a Club Med and were powerfully attracted to each other. They both recalled their first sexual encounter with each other as the most amazing experience of their lives. They were in their early thirties at the time, and they'd both had plenty of sexual experience—but nothing like what they experienced with each other. There was a "depth," as Phyllis described it, to that sexual encounter that made all the sex she had experienced up until then seem flat. Their sex life continued to have this incredibly powerful quality even after they returned to Chicago, where they both lived. Phyllis moved into Wayne's condo, and within a month they were married. The sex continued to be great.

The first signs of trouble appeared when they began looking for a condo to buy jointly. When they found a condo he liked she'd hate it, and vice versa. When they came home from these frustrating house-hunting trips their dinners were silent, but once they got into the bedroom they could connect again, and the sex continued to be wonderful—most of the time. There started to be occasions when the sex was just OK. Neither had been expecting sex that was just OK with this particular partner, certainly not this early in the marriage.

For a number of months, Phyllis and Wayne spent virtually all their free time looking for a condo until they finally found one that neither hated. Realizing that this would be the best they could do, they bought it. They then spent most of their free time over the next several months fixing it and furnishing it—and disagreeing about almost everything. They disagreed about which improvements to make and how to finance them, and they disagreed about how to decorate the condo—from the carpets to the lighting fixtures and everything in between. Phyllis and Wayne continued to have fabulous sex most of the time, but the episodes of just-OK sex were becoming more frequent.

Their sex life deteriorated quite rapidly after they had completed their work on the condo: Their just-OK sexual encounters became the rule rather than the exception, and their sexual frequency started to go down. They found themselves either "too tired" or "not in the mood." In their last six months together they didn't have sex even once. At the time they broke up, they had been married barely two years.

In individual therapy with Phyllis after the breakup, we were able to reconstruct what had happened: As long as Phyllis and Wayne were involved with the condo, they were involved with each other. Even though a lot of their interaction was conflictual, they at least felt their partner to be an emotional presence in their life. But once that was over they became emotionally disengaged from each other. Their differences on the Practical Dimension kept Phyllis and Wayne irritated with each other on a daily basis, but these spats about day-to-day life didn't have the scale and significance to keep them engaged with each other, as their arguments over the condo had. And because Phyllis and Wayne had so little in common on the Wavelength Dimension, they had nothing to talk about when they weren't quarreling, and they felt more and more distant from each other. Eventually their lack of a nonsexual relationship made their sexual relationship, wonderful as it had been, impossible.

Practical-Only

This, I believe, is the next most common One-Dimensional marriage. It's a marriage of convenience. People who get into this kind of marriage do so almost exclusively because of the pressure to get married: It's time to get married and start a family, and this person will do. In the best case, their children serve as a focus for some sense of togetherness. But if one of the partners has any degree of yearning for sexual companionship, or emotional and spiritual companionship, he or she starts to feel dead in the marriage, children or not, and wants to get out. Sometimes it takes finding a new partner for the unsatisfied spouse to get out, but often it does not because the desire to be independent and feel like oneself again is motivation enough.

Julius and Consuela had a Practical-Only marriage that didn't last. Julius was forty when they met and Consuela was twenty-five. Julius had, by then, experienced many passionate and tumultuous relationships, and he felt ready to settle down. Consuela was ready to get married, too. Although she had a good job as a paralegal, what she really wanted was to be a mother. Consuela was a strikingly beautiful woman and her beauty was what initially drew Julius to her. He was also charmed by what he called "her gentle innocence." Consuela's understanding of relationships, and of life in general, was refreshingly sunny and simple to Julius, whose own view of things was much more dark and complex. Consuela saw Julius as a wise older man—as much a teacher as a lover—who would take care of her but who needed a woman's care himself.

Julius and Consuela had been involved for a year when his firm offered him a one-year transfer to Hong Kong. It was a great opportunity, and Julius wanted Consuela to go with him. Consuela said she would, if he would marry her. This threw Julius into a quandary. He appreciated the legitimacy of Consuela's position—she'd been clear early on about her desire to marry—but he had developed second thoughts about marrying her. Although he was still charmed by Consuela's "gentle innocence" he was beginning to find it irritating at times. More important, Julius was dissatisfied with their sexual relationship. At first, he had assumed that Consuela would become more comfortable with him sexually as they got to know each other better, but that did not happen. By the end of their first year together, Julius was still waiting for his sexual relationship with Consuela to be as passionate and satisfying as the sex he'd experienced with previous partners. On the other hand, he was convinced that Consuela would be a great wife and mother, and he'd developed a detailed fantasy of how pleasant having a family with Consuela could be. Finally Julius decided, as he put it, "to be optimistic about the relationship." They married and moved to Hong Kong.

The first year of the marriage was fine, largely because of the excitement of being in Hong Kong, but once they returned home things started going downhill. The fact was that Julius and Consuela were so different in their outlook that they didn't have much to say to each other. And they had major disagreements about issues related to their values, especially about how much in the way of money and possessions they needed in order to be happy. Almost immediately after their first child arrived, Julius and Consuela were arguing about what the child needed to have a good life. It was only after their second child was in kindergarten that they decided they had to separate. It was the first important life choice they had agreed upon in years. Their divorce was rancorous, which is not surprising considering their many years of mutual disapproval and resentment. But ultimately their story had a happy ending, of sorts:

Within about a year of their divorce each of them met someone who was much closer to them on the Wavelength Dimension, and with whom they could have the kind of sexual relationship they wanted.

Sometimes people who are unhappy in a Practical-Only marriage never get out, and the consequences can be ugly: Every once in a while, I am referred a middle-aged couple who have been married for twenty years or more and report that they have been unhappy the whole time. By the time the two partners get to my office they aren't just angry at each other; they *hate* each other. Trapped in their Practical-Only marriage, each sees the other as having withheld from them the most important comforts—sexual and emotional companionship—that marriage is supposed to offer. But it's not that the partners were withholding those comforts. They were just too different to be able to offer those comforts to each other.

Wavelength-Only

These marriages are quite rare, I think. The people who enter into them believe that friendship is enough. As you know by now, I believe that friendship is at the core of any happy and intimate marriage—but it is not enough. The two friends who get married find that conflict about how to live day by day is wearing on their relationship. And eventually one or both of them may realize that to live together without a sexual bond is a barren experience. If that happens, they end the marriage so that they can remain friends.

Two-Dimensional Marriages

My belief is that the largest number of American marriages are Two-Dimensional marriages of one combination or another. These marriages can range from workable and OK to tempestuous but happy. Many of these marriages stay intact; many others don't.

Wavelength/Practical

This kind of marriage has everything but sex. If sex is not very important to either partner, they can both be happy in the marriage because they are best friends and they get along well. But if sex is important at all to one of the partners, that person will be unhappy, feeling that life is passing him or her by. The sexually uninterested partner may know nothing about the other's sexual frustration. Or they may know about it but don't want to know it because they feel there is nothing they can do about it. Sometimes, the sexually interested one addresses the problem forthrightly and tries by various means (maybe even marital therapy) to develop the other's interest in sex, but this rarely works. The sexually interested one then drops overt discussion of the issue, and the uninterested one tries to believe that since the other partner is no longer talking about sex, it is no longer a problem.

But of course it is. Sometimes the sexually interested partner simply lives out the rest of the marriage in a state of sexual frustration because he or she will not go outside the marriage for sex—either for principled, moral reasons or because of anxiety and fear. Sometimes, of course, the sexually interested partner does go outside the marriage for sex. If this extramarital sex is strictly sex, it can stabilize the marriage (which is not to say that I endorse it, but it *can* serve that function). Sometimes that extramarital sex is even conducted with the tacit approval of the sexually uninterested partner, because it relieves the guilt over not being able to fulfill the other's sexual needs. There is always the risk, though, that the partner who goes outside the marriage will fall in love with the new sexual companion, and that, naturally, does destabilize the marriage.

Sex may be so important to you that it's hard for you to conceive of a satisfying Wavelength/Practical marriage. They do exist—when the partners match in their lack of need for sex. Horace and Colleen are an example. He is a librarian and she is a high school English teacher, so it's not surprising that they met at a writers' workshop. As they got to know each other, they came to realize that they were very much on the same wavelength. They developed a deep fondness for each other, and after several months of close companionship they realized that they had fallen in love. They decided to get married.

Although Horace and Colleen were in their late thirties, neither of them had dated much and neither had much sexual experience. Actually, neither had ever been very interested in sex or comfortable with it.

Horace and Colleen conducted a chaste courtship that didn't progress beyond affectionate touching and kissing. As they both had feared, their wedding night did not go well. For a while afterward they struggled to establish a full sexual relationship, but because of their inhibitions it didn't work and only led to awkwardness and tension between them. Finally, they leveled with each other and told each other how they felt about sex. Each was relieved to discover that the other would be perfectly satisfied with a marriage that didn't have the pressure of sexual expectations. They continued their marriage on that basis, lived harmoniously from day to day, and continued to be each other's best friend. And, because each of them had always dreamed of having a child, they adopted one and raised him into a fine (and, ironically, sexually confident) young man.

Practical/Sex

My guess is that this is the most common type of Two-Dimensional marriage. The partners get along in their everyday life, and they maintain a good sexual bond. How happy they are depends on what they were expecting from marriage. If they really weren't expecting deep companionship— if they feel that deep companionship is not to be expected from marriage, or if they know that they cannot expect deep companionship with their partner but value each other in many other ways—then they can feel quite happy. They derive a sense of close companionship from their family of origin, from their same-sex friends, and from the community groups they are part of. And they feel companionship with each other because of their children. The children are what they uniquely have in common with each other and with no one else.

The people who tend to be the happiest in these marriages are the ones who define marriage in terms of traditional gender roles: husband as provider, wife as homemaker. The partners carry out their assigned tasks and everything runs smoothly; they are each more focused on their children than on each other. They see themselves primarily as being part of a close and loving *family* rather than as part of a close and intimate marital relationship. But traditional gender roles are not required for a happy Practical/Sex marriage. Partners who enact nontraditional gender roles can also have a fine Practical/Sex marriage. Kent and Ellie are an example.

Kent and Ellie met, as many avid skiers do, on the slopes. At the moment they met, they were the only two people at the top of a challenging, superadvanced trail. Soon they found out that they both also loved snorkeling and scuba diving. They spent a series of vacations and long weekends engaging in these low-conversation activities during the day and making passionate love at night. Each found the other very easy to get along with. Planning their trips always went smoothly, and when they were together they found themselves very in sync: They always seemed to want to do the same thing at the same time.

Kent, an engineer, managed to find a job in the city where Ellie worked as the features editor of a newspaper. They moved in together and were delighted to find that they could live as harmoniously with each other when they weren't on vacation as when they were. They married and have had a congenial life together for many years.

Only they're not on the same wavelength. Kent does not share Ellie's artistic and intellectual interests. She can't have the kinds of deep conversations with Kent that she can have with her friends at the newspaper and in the city's cultural community. It's not that Kent isn't willing to listen; he just doesn't have a lot to say about the cultural topics that are closest to Ellie's heart. About ten years into their marriage, Kent and Ellie even gave up on going to the movies together, because neither enjoyed the movies that the other preferred. (Well, they actually still do *go* to the movies together—to a multiplex, where he sees his movie and she sees hers.) Kent is a committed churchgoer, Ellie isn't, and he's generally somewhat more conservative than she is on social and political issues.

Kent doesn't seem to miss deep conversations with Ellie. He adores her and greatly enjoys her company, and they've had plenty to talk about concerning the raising of their two daughters. Ellie is more ambivalent. On the one hand, she feels lonely at times. She wishes that she could have deep conversations with Kent and feel that kind of closeness with him, and she is envious when she encounters couples who do have that closeness. On the other hand, she believes that Kent's mysterious otherness is part of what's kept him such a powerful sexual turn-on for her over the years.

Partners in Practical/Sex marriages may wonder from time to time, Is this all there is?—especially the wife, when she reads about love and relationships in magazines or self-help books. Not surprisingly, these marriages can be hit particularly hard by the "empty nest syndrome" once the children grow up and leave home, and some of them don't last beyond that point. But many others do last, with the partners' overall experience ranging from the contentment that Kent and Ellie feel to what Thoreau called "quiet desperation."

Wavelength/Sex

These are tempestuous marriages where the partners fight all the time, but it's clear that they deeply love each other. These couples usually don't seek marital therapy, even though their marriages are conflict ridden. They don't because they are happy in their marriage; there is no one else in the world they would rather be with. Her chronic lateness may drive him nuts, just as his persistent inability to get his dirty underwear into the hamper drives her nuts. He wants the music loud; she wants it soft—or even better, off. Next to her and the kids, he loves the dog most of all. She can't figure out how he could cuddle and commune with that dirty, smelly creature. As far as the kids are concerned, they'll fight about some things that are related to their own differences in modus vivendi, such as how late the kids can stay up. But on many other things pertaining to the kids they will agree, since raising kids is largely a matter of values—and being on the same wavelength, they will generally share the same values.

In Wavelength/Sex marriages, there are endless spats about all sorts of day-to-day things. Over a very long time, the partners may be able to get a little closer to each other on the Practical Dimension. If they don't, their never-ending conflict and chronic anger can be wearing on both of them. But despite the undercurrent of exasperation and anger, they remain each other's best friend and passionate lover.

Trudi and Hank are an example. They met in their early twenties, on their first day of graduate school. As soon as they laid eyes on each other, at the party for incoming students, each knew instinctively that they had met the great love of their lives. They were right. (That kind of mutual recognition does sometimes happen when people are closely matched sexually and are on the same wavelength.) By the end of their second semester Trudi and Hank were married, ecstatic—and fighting. They fought over just about everything. They shared the housework and rotated tasks in their equal marriage, and both felt it was a fair arrangement, but neither approved of how the other got things done. When Hank cleaned up the kitchen, it wasn't clean enough for Trudi. When she did the food shopping she always forgot to get something important, including items that were important to her. When Hank shopped, it was overkill—or so said Trudi. She didn't like the way he folded laundry and he didn't like the way she did it. He didn't worry about money and she did. The list of their differences was almost endless. To make matters worse, each of them had an explosive temper, so that whenever there was a difference, there was an explosion. Their fights were over almost as quickly as they began, though, and they would get right back to an intense conversation about whatever they were both passionately interested in at the moment. And if they found themselves angry with each other at bedtime, sex was a cure for that. By the time I met Hank and Trudi (as social acquaintances, not clients) they had been married ten years and had a couple of kids. Although their rate of fighting had tapered off a bit, by their own admission it was still high.

Couples who are far apart on the Practical Dimension can be very happy, as Hank and Trudi have been for many years. But there is one qualification: No matter how different the partners in a Wavelength/Sex marriage are on various aspects of the Practical Dimension, they have to agree on one important thing on that dimension: what *model of marriage* they want to follow. As you will see in chapter 9, if they don't agree on that, they won't be happy.

COMPARING Practical/Sex marriages with Wavelength/Sex marriages highlights the importance of the Wavelength Dimension in having a happy marriage. People in Practical/Sex marriages have workable relationships, but they may or may not be happy. People in Wavelength/Sex marriages are more likely to be happy, because the element of close companionship is there along with the sex, and this combination enables the couple to get over the rough spots caused by their incompatibility on the Practical Dimension.

In Part Two, when I go into detail about each of the compatibility dimensions, I hope you'll pay particular attention to the Wavelength Dimension, since it is so important to feeling emotionally close and happy in your marriage.

6

FILLING IN THE DETAILS: YOUR (MY) QUESTIONS ANSWERED

In conveying my message to you so far I have taken the shortest, most direct route—no stops, no detours, no side trips. You've seen the landscape in its overall contours, but some details were blurry; and there are some features of the landscape that you haven't been able to see at all. As a result, along the way some questions may have occurred to you.

This chapter makes the stops and the side trips. It discusses in more detail some of the points made earlier. And it considers points that haven't been brought up at all so far. I've used a question/answer format for this. Some of my questions may well match some of yours.

1. You say that good communication skills and conflict resolution skills are not the essential ingredient for a happy marriage. Do you mean that they are of no value?

No. They are of great value in any marriage, because even in happy marriages there is conflict. And it's easier for any two people to resolve conflict if they listen to each other carefully without interrupting, show each other that they have understood what the other has said, and keep themselves from making hostile accusations and calling each other names. The more conflict there is in a relationship, the more frequently these skills will come into play, and if the partners use them life will go along easier. But in a marriage with a great deal of conflict, where the partners see most things very differently, that's about all these skills will do—make life go along easier. In the absence of similarity between the partners on the Three Dimensions of Compatibility, these skills are not enough to fuel the process of mutual affirmation necessary for lasting love.

Imagine two contrasting couples: Alan and Allison have very poor communication skills, but they are very close to each other on the compatibility dimensions. Barry and Barbara are the opposite. They have great communication skills, but they are far apart on the compatibility dimensions. What are their lives like?

Alan and Allison agree on most things about how to lead their lives, they enjoy a lot of activities together, they find each other endlessly interesting to talk to, and they enjoy each other in bed. Every once in a while, though, a disagreement comes up and they fight. They fight dirty—yelling and screaming, interrupting each other, and calling each other names. Alan and Allison may stay angry at each other for a few hours, or maybe even a day or two. But they don't stay angry at each other too long because they value each other too much. They cool down and resolve the conflict. Or they just drop it without resolving it, which is just fine because in a lot of marital conflicts, what is needed is not resolution but simply for the conflict to be aired. (Example: Allison asks Alan to buy some plane tickets while a limited-time discount is being offered. Alan gets involved in something else he deems important and forgets to buy the tickets before the offer expires. Allison gets angry at Alan and asks him how he could be so stupid as to miss the deadline. Alan, feeling very guilty and angry at himself, gets defensively angry at Allison. He tells her that the next time something like this comes up she should take care of it, since she's Miss Perfect. Allison angrily replies that if Mr. Screwup can't take care of it, then Miss Perfect most definitely will. And that's the end of the conversation. There was nothing to resolve—the discounted tickets were already lost—but the emotions were aired. And next time something like this comes up, Allison *will* ask Alan to take care of it. And he *will* take care of it because, as Allison well knows, he generally does.) Alan and Allison get past the conflict and go back to affirming each other in all the ways they do because they are so similar to each other. They get right back to loving each other. Would Alan and Allison's marriage be better, happier, even, if they had better communication and conflict resolution skills? Sure! If they had those skills, then they would feel respected and affirmed during the 5 percent of the time they are in conflict, as well as during the 95 percent when they are getting along just fine.

Barry and Barbara don't have a lot in common. There's not a lot they like to do together, they don't find each other very interesting, they don't have a lot to say to each other, and they don't have much of a sex life. But they do have great communication skills. Whenever they are in conflict, which is pretty often, since they disagree on so many things, they are very polite about it. They sit down at the kitchen table, listen to each other attentively, and never interrupt or insult each other. Whether they resolve the conflict or simply agree to disagree, they do it gently and in a way that is mutually affirming. But that's just about the only way they are mutually affirming, because they are so different from each other. Are their communication and conflict resolution skills enough for them to have a *happy* marriage, as opposed to a marriage that is merely smooth-running? I don't think so. Or look at it this way: Whose marriage would you rather be in, Alan and Allison's, or Barry and Barbara's?

Writers of marital self-help books go from saying that there is conflict in all marriages to saying that the essential ingredients for happy marriage are good communication and problem-solving skills. In doing this they are making three mistakes. The first mistake is the logical error of arguing that because two things are correlated, one of them causes the other. That is, they are saying that good communication causes happy marriage simply because the two seem to go together. But just because two things go together does not mean that one is the cause of the other. For example, we might find a high correlation between the number of hours between sundown and sunrise and the amount of money people spend—that is, more nighttime hours, more spending. But it would be a mistake to say that longer nights cause increased spending, since the period between Thanksgiving and Christmas, when most people do a tremendous amount of spending, happens to occur when the nights are becoming longest. *If there is any causal relationship between happiness and communication in marriage—which so far has not been proven—it may well be that marital happiness causes good communication rather than vice versa.*

The second mistake these writers make is that in saying that there is always conflict, which is undeniable, they overlook the fact that *how much* conflict there is makes a huge difference. And the amount of conflict in a marriage does not depend principally on the couple's communication skills (although vicious circles of conflict about conflict can and do happen), but on how similar or different the partners are on the major dimensions of compatibility. If the partners are compatible, there isn't that much conflict, since they spontaneously agree most of the time.

The third and most important mistake these writers make is to confuse marriages that are workable with marriages that are *happy*. Workable marriages and happy marriages are not the same thing; many workable marriages are not happy. Have you ever noticed how often experts on marriage talk about marriages as if they were structures—buildings or highway overpasses—rather than as something involving human beings and their emotions? They use words like "sound," "solid," and "strong" to describe good marriages. When I hear people talk like that, I wonder what ever happened to happiness as the measure of marriage. I sometimes wonder if these writers have simply given up on happiness, real happiness, as being possible in marriage. But happiness *is* possible in marriage, and that's what we should be aiming for—not just a marriage that's like an adequately constructed piece of civil engineering.

2. If you say that the level of compatibility between two people cannot be changed, and I'm in an unhappy marriage, are you saying that it's hopeless—that I should throw in the towel and find someone else?

No, not at all. Marriages can have problems for other reasons than the partners' being incompatible. The first thing you and your partner have to do is determine whether or not your problems stem mainly from incompatibility. You can do that, of course, by working through this book together. If your assessment is that you and your partner *are* compatible enough, then you have to identify what other factors are causing problems in the marriage. (If you can't identify those other factors yourselves, a marital therapist will be able to help you.) Once you've identified them, then you can read one of the better books on marital communication and problem solving, and use the techniques you learn there to help you solve the problem. It might even be that the problem is simply poor communication skills. That is sometimes the case.

If, on the contrary, it turns out that your problems are indeed due to incompatibility, it's still not hopeless. You can get a book called *Reconcilable Differences* (see "For Further Reading" at the back of this book). Written by two leading clinician/researchers in marital therapy, Andrew Christensen and Neil S. Jacobson, the book is designed specifically to help partners accept and tolerate their incompatibilities, and, if at all possible, build bridges across them. You can work through that book together, trying the various techniques recommended in it. And again, if at any point you don't feel you can do it yourself, you can hire a marital therapist to help you.

Only after you've gone through that process of exploration, awareness, and experimentation will it be time for you to decide if you can get enough of what you most need and want from your marriage. Specifically, you'll be able to determine if you and your partner, giving it your best effort, have been able to achieve a marriage that is happy or one that is just workable. If you've been able to fashion a marriage that is workable but not really happy, it will then be up to you to decide whether that's good enough for you over the long term.

The decision to separate and divorce is complex and difficult, and it is based on many considerations other than personal happiness—religious commitments, economic factors, and concerns about the effects of separation and divorce on the children, to name just a few. Because of these considerations, people sometimes choose to stay in unhappy marriages.

3. You say that compatibility is the key to a happy marriage. Yet you say that you came up with your ideas about compati-

bility from treating well-matched couples who had marital problems. If they were so well matched, why did they show up at your office? Why did they have marital problems?

The answer is that there are lots of ways that people can be unhappy. Sometimes life throws the couple a huge challenge, and it can overwhelm their ability to cope. Sometimes one of the partners, or both, can have an individual problem that causes problems in the marriage, no matter how compatible they are. And every once in a while, a well-matched couple can find themselves hung up on just one or two narrowly focused conflicts. Let me give you some examples.

Ed and Diana got married in their late thirties and were worried about fertility problems, so they didn't waste time trying to have kids. To their great joy, they had no trouble conceiving their first child, a girl. A couple of years later they figured it was time for their daughter to have a little brother or sister, and to their delight they had no trouble conceiving a little brother for her. And then, within just a few months of his birth, they conceived another little brother for her. They were not exactly delighted this last time because they had planned on having only two children.

By the time Ed and Diana came to see me, their kids were five, two, and one. It quickly became clear that Ed and Diana's problem was that the kids had crowded out their own interpersonal relationship. It was not just that the kids required a lot of work; as a matter of fact, Ed and Diana handled that part quite well. The problem was that Ed and Diana had allowed the kids to intrude on their couple relationship in ways that could have been prevented. Bedtimes were always a problem, and too often either Ed or Diana would end up falling asleep at night with one of the children. Guess what that did to their sex life? They hadn't cleared a space for their relationship, in other ways. They hardly ever went out together in the evening, and they had *never* taken a weekend alone together since the birth of their first child.

It's not only kids that get in the way of marital relationships. Jobs often do, especially high-powered ones. Stuart was in a fast-track corporate job, and Pattie was working long hours to make partner in a major law firm. They both worked late into the evening, and they often worked on weekends. When they were able to spend time together, they were generally preoccupied, anxious, and exhausted. Their presenting complaint was that the "sparkle has gone out of our marriage." Surprise.

Sometimes people overwhelm themselves to an amazing degree. Bryna and Woody were trying to develop their bakery business, remodel their house (doing much of the work themselves), and raise their infant twins *all at the same time*. They were in an equal marriage, which served them very well in some respects but left them with fluid roles. The result was that there was confusion and conflict from day to day—even from hour to hour—about who should be doing what.

Other stressors can cause a couple's model of marriage to break down. Joe and Mary were in their fifties when I met them. Their traditional gender roles had worked well for both of them for many years, even though Mary worked as a nurse in addition to having primary responsibility for the housework. But when her disabled mother moved in with them, it became too much. Mary asked Joe for help, but he didn't give it to her because she had "taken care of everything" up to then, and anyway it was *her* mother.

We all know that being laid off, being unemployed, or having financial problems can cause conflict, even among the most well-matched couples.

Tragedies also can lead well-matched, happy couples to have conflict. I've treated a number of couples with fertility problems, who have gone through the long, grueling process of trying to get pregnant with medical help and did not succeed. These couples are frustrated and grief-stricken. The eroticism has been leached out of their sex life by all the scheduled, programmed intercourse they've had to do. And now they're facing the question of adoption, which is almost always difficult.

Now, for the individual problems that can harm the marital relationship: The most frequent is alcoholism. Caitlin and Morris's story is one of thousands that are exactly the same. They loved each other deeply, but he was an alcoholic. He was physically absent a lot, drinking, and when he was home he was emotionally absent much of the time because he was drunk or hungover. Of course, he denied all this. Once he phoned me to change an appointment and his speech was obviously slurred. He denied that, too.

Sometimes, one partner can have a mental disorder that causes great problems. For example, Colin had a Bipolar II disorder that went undiagnosed for many years. Bipolar II disorder is a type of manic depression in which the manic phase—which can be the person's usual state—is not psychotic. The person with Bipolar II looks normal enough at first glance; certainly there is none of the incoherent talk, agitation, and bizarre behavior that characterize full-blown mania. Rather, the person's behavior is abnormal in more subtle ways. He or she can be, for example, grandiose, impulsive, irritable, and prone to very bad judgment. These features in Colin, over the years, had wrought havoc in his marriage with Serena, and his last get-rich-quick scheme landed them in bankruptcy. Finally, Colin was correctly diagnosed—Bipolar II disorder was just beginning to be understood at the time—and put on lithium. He changed radically as a result, and for the first time recognized how much damage he had done to himself and to the woman he loved so much. And despite the bankruptcy, Serena was happier than she had ever been in her marriage with him.

The partner's individual disorder doesn't have to be a diagnosable, psychiatric syndrome to cause major problems. Blake's father was a good and kind man, except that when he got into conflict with his wife he became psychologically brutal and sadistic, almost as if he enjoyed running her down. By some combination of nature and nurture, Blake had the same nasty streak, despite being a good and kind man otherwise. Although he and his wife, Sheila, were very well matched and loved each other deeply, Blake's mean streak made the marriage impossible for her.

Jonathan's problem was of a very different kind. He'd been repeatedly shuttled from one of his divorced parents to the other, causing him to feel abandoned by both. Along the way he had learned too well that children should be seen and not heard, and that what should be especially not heard is anything in the way of a request, much less a complaint. As a result, in his relationship with Shirley—with whom he was wonderfully well matched, and who was warm and nurturing to boot—he was simply afraid to make requests or express complaints. So he wouldn't express himself—until he felt so pent up that he would explode in a fit of anger, which he experienced as being out of his control. (Notice that even in the case of this communicatively challenged man, the problem wasn't so much being unskilled in communication as it was simply being afraid.) Once he got over his fear, his and Shirley's marriage was able to reach its full potential for happiness.

These are just a few of the individual problems that a partner can bring into the marriage. There are many more. The origins of some of these problems can be traced back to negative events in childhood—for example, problems with trust and sexuality because of early experiences of abuse. The origins of others cannot be traced with any confidence. The problems are just there, causing conflict in the marriage no matter how closely matched the partners are.

Partners don't have to be suffering from individual psychological problems to find themselves in serious conflict over some narrowly defined issue. All they have to do is make a mistake in communication and problem solving and they can get locked into a power struggle that's very damaging. The issue can be just about anything, as long as the partners consider it to be important. In chapter 13 I'll be giving you a couple of examples of such conflicts and how they were resolved.

Finally, couples can have problems specifically because they are well matched. Especially if the partners married young, before they were all grown up and able to cope with life's challenges independently, they run the risk of being *too* close: too involved in each other's lives; too dependent on each other (and no one else) for companionship, conversation, recreation, emotional support—everything. If they hermetically seal themselves in their marriage in this way, one or both of them will come to feel smothered, limited, and sexually turned off. In order to solve this problem, the partners have to back off from each other, allow other people into their lives, and reestablish their own personal independence.

4. Can't incompatibilities develop between partners who were originally compatible, because they have different experiences and because their circumstances change?

Conflicts can certainly arise, *but conflicts are not the same thing as incompatibilities.* The textbook example of "incompatibilities" developing during the course of a marriage generally involves a woman's self-actualization. Read this example of that kind of textbook case:

> Personal experiences in each partner's work world or social world apart from the other may create new needs and desires that conflict with the partner's. For example, Ann and Daren may have been compatible on issues of closeness and time together throughout their courtship and early marriage. However, later in the relationship, Ann makes an important career change that moves her into a demanding but exciting position. She spends long hours at the office and no longer has the time for Daren that she used to have.[1]

Now read it again, carefully, and make sure that you haven't read too much into it. Did you, by any chance, jump to the conclusion that, because of her new job, Ann cares less about Daren than she used to?

Let's think about the example together and try to imagine how Ann and Daren would be *feeling* in that situation. (Notice that the example didn't say anything about how Ann and Daren felt about her long work hours at the office.) The story implies that for quite some time Ann and Daren enjoyed spending a lot of time together. Then Ann gets the new job and doesn't have time for Daren anymore. A reader might conclude from this that the lack of time together is a problem for Daren but not for Ann—that it is a conflict *between* them. But if Ann and Daren are well matched on the Wavelength Dimension, then her long work hours, and her time away from Daren, are not just a problem for him; they're a problem for her, too. She misses spending time with him, and she feels guilty about depriving Daren of time with her. Ann's new job has put her *in conflict with herself*. Daren is in conflict with *himself*, too. He misses the time that he and Ann used to spend together. But at the same time, being on the same wavelength as Ann, he supports her commitment to her new job. He may even feel guilty about asking her to cut down on her work hours to spend time with him. So, Ann's time commitment is not a brand-new incompatibility between them—it's just a problem. It causes as much conflict *within* each of them as it causes between them—maybe more. They will devise a solution to it that will work for both of them, because

Ann doesn't value her time with Daren any less than she ever did, and because Daren affirms Ann's career aspirations.

Now imagine the same situation, but this time imagine that Ann has never really felt she was on the same wavelength as Daren. She never felt really interested in him, or stimulated by him, as a person. She spent a lot of time with Daren and it was fun, pretty much, but then again she had nothing more fulfilling to do. Then Ann gets the new job. The job is interesting and stimulating, and she feels affirmed there in ways she never felt affirmed with Daren. So she spends a lot of time at work, and she doesn't particularly miss those long hours she had spent with Daren. In this case, Ann is not in conflict with herself—just with Daren. And, in this case, we are justified in saying that her long hours at work are an expression of an incompatibility between the two of them. But it is an incompatibility that was there all along. It's just that Ann and Daren were not able to perceive it clearly until Ann became more self-actualized.

Let me give you another example of how conflict that emerges as the partners become more self-actualized is not the same thing as incompatibility. It is a personal example, and it makes Ann and Daren's problem look like a piece of cake. One day in the spring of 1993, my wife got a phone call from the University of Chicago. The call was to tell her that its anthropology department had just voted to make her a full professor there. The call came out of nowhere; neither of us had been expecting it. Sue had certainly not been looking for a job there.

The University of Chicago's anthropology department has been the top-rated department in the country for decades. Being invited to join it is, for an anthropologist, the equivalent of being nominated to the Supreme Court. But that's what happens when you are as smart, hard-working, and dedicated as Sue is. (At the time, Sue was a member of the anthropology department at Rutgers University. Rutgers is a great school, but its anthropology department is not ranked as highly as Chicago's.)[2]

So, being invited to the University of Chicago was a great honor and a great opportunity for Sue. The only problem was that I was well established in private practice in New Jersey, having worked hard to build that practice over thirteen years. For me, moving to Chicago would mean either finding some kind of job, which didn't appeal to me after so many

years of being my own boss, or else starting all over again in private practice there, which would be difficult. Plus, New Jersey was home to me; I
really didn't want to move to Chicago. As a result, Sue and I spent a year
in conflict about whether to move. But this conflict was not the develop-
ment of an incompatibility between us. Nothing had changed in terms of
how important Sue's job was to her, or mine to me, compared with our
relationship. Each of us was very committed to our career, *and each of us
didn't want the other to be hurt, or our relationship to be hurt, by whatever
decision we made.* In other words, each of us was in as much conflict
within ourselves as we were with each other. It took us almost a year to
make the decision to move, and it was not easy. But during that whole
tense time we understood each other because of our compatibility, and so
we were able to empathize with each other's desires even when they were
opposed to our own.

When couples start out close on the compatibility dimensions, they
stay close. Conflicts inevitably develop but they are not incompatibilities.
Conflicts are incompatibility only when the partners were incompatible in
the first place.

**5. You say that respect in marriage is based on mutual under-
standing, which in turn is based on similarity on the compatibility dimensions. But shouldn't people respect each other no
matter what?**

They should but they don't. In this way, as in so many others, the
world as it really exists is different from what we'd like it to be. It's not
psychologically realistic for people who don't understand each other to be
able to respect what they don't understand. Imagine Frank and Felicia.
Frank is an ardent environmentalist who believes that forests should not
be cut down if that will endanger some rare species of bird. Felicia
believes that jobs are more important than birds. In her view, the forests
should be cut, even if it means wiping out the birds, because that is what
is necessary for an entire group of people to be able to continue to support
their families. Frank and Felicia are each likely to be thinking about the

other, "How can he/she possibly think like that?" which is just a short step away from, "What's wrong with him/her?" If you are having these thoughts about your partner, it's very unlikely that you'll also be thinking, "But I really respect him/her for having that nutso opinion." It's not logically impossible for people to think these three things all at once, but it doesn't happen. People are not constructed that way, psychologically. Frank and Felicia would have had a much easier time respecting each other if they had both been devoted to birds or to jobs.

Now, unfortunately, it does not follow that being similar to your partner on the compatibility dimensions guarantees that your partner will respect you. If your partner is one of those people who has to feel superior to everyone, including their mate, then they will find things to put you down about no matter how compatible you are. In this restricted way, respect is a matter of moral character and not similarity: A partner of poor moral character may not respect you even though you two are compatible enough for the respect between you to be mutual.

6. You seem to be saying that people often pick their marriage partners for reasons that are relatively superficial, conventional, and socially determined. But don't people pick their marriage partners for deep, unconscious, psychological reasons stemming from psychic wounds they suffered in childhood?

No, they don't—at least not the vast majority of us, who are basically in good mental health. We don't because we're not wounded. This may come as a surprise to you, because many people claim that we're all wounded. But that just isn't so. The fact is, *resilience,* rather than vulnerability, is the rule in the way that both adults and children react to adversity and trauma. Most children who experience traumatic events or substandard parenting do not show lasting psychic scars as a result.[3]

The research on children of divorce, for example, provides strong evidence for resilience. Parental divorce is experienced as highly traumatic by most children. And children of divorce have higher rates of adjustment problems in their adulthood than children from nondivorced families. But it is only a small minority of children of divorce who bear these lasting scars. The rest, in the words of a major authority on this subject, "develop into reasonably competent individuals functioning within the normal range of adjustment."[4] If traumas like divorce don't leave psychic wounds on most children, it would be surprising if less traumatic adversities did. (My favorite version of "We are all wounded" is that we men—privileged as we are in so many ways—are nevertheless wounded because we were taught not to express our emotions as we were growing up. Give me a break!)

It is true that some people who have been traumatized, and who have suffered lasting wounds as a result, choose their spouses based on those wounds. For example, a woman who had been repeatedly raped by her father once told me, "I married Jim because I knew he'd never hurt me." And even people who have not quite been traumatized by their parents' mistreatment of them pick their mates with the memory of that mistreatment in mind.

People with major psychological problems do seem to pick their mates based on those problems more than mentally healthy people do. It is clear, for example, that people with serious, chronic mood disorders marry each other at higher rates than would be expected by chance. It's easy to see why. When people are unlucky enough to be chronically depressed—especially if the depression started in early childhood, as it frequently does—the depression colors all aspects of their outlook: how they view themselves, how they view the world, how they experience interpersonal relationships, how they think about the future. So when two chronically depressed people meet each other, they often find that they have a high level of mutual understanding based on their shared misfortune. (It should be noted, by the way, that this misfortune is overwhelmingly genetic in origin and not the result of maltreatment by parents.) They find themselves on the same wavelength in ways that they couldn't with someone who had not suffered from lifelong depression. But even among these people whose lives and outlook have been dominated by their mental problems, only a small minority are attracted to each other and get married on that basis.

The moral of the story is that for the rest of us, who are basically mentally healthy, and whose psychological hang-ups are comparatively small-scale and do not have a major influence on our behavior and outlook, it's highly unlikely that our choice of mate will be determined by those hang-ups. Especially when you consider all the other bases on which we can be attracted to each other, and decide to marry each other, the idea that our hang-ups could override all of them is implausible.

You are right about what I seemed to be saying. Just as we human beings are resilient, we are flexible. We are flexible enough to find a great variety of people attractive enough to fall in love with and to marry. That flexibility interacts with conventional, socially determined considerations, plus a large dose of chance, to determine whom we end up marrying.

7. In your description of the compatibility dimensions, you don't say anything about people's personalities. Psychic wounds aside, don't people's personalities have to match for them to be compatible?

This is a very important question, and a complicated one. The short answer to it is yes, in a sense, people's personalities have to match up for them to be compatible. But the full answer is long and it has several parts:

a) First, let's get straight on what we mean by "personality." What we mean is consistency in the person's behavior across a variety of situations in which some specific personality trait could come into play. In fact, we don't see the person's personality trait directly, because that trait, whatever it is—"honest," "neat," "persistent," et cetera—is simply a generalization we make from watching that person in a variety of situations. So, if we notice that a man's house is always tidy, that his clothing is always pressed, that there's never a scrap of paper in his car, and that his workbench is never cluttered, then we call that man "neat." If he is neat in some situations but not in others—when there isn't that level of consistency in his behavior—we might not be inclined to say that being neat is one of the chief features of his personality.

Sometimes it is convenient and informative to describe ourselves and others by using personality descriptions, but sometimes it is better to talk in terms of specific behaviors in specific situations. For example, it is convenient and informative to describe people as neat if they are consistently neat. And it is helpful to think about yourself and your partner in personality terms for some other components of the Practical Dimension. But it's hard to find one word that describes other aspects of people—the various attitudes and habits that people have concerning money, for example. It's easier to talk about specific behaviors, such as saving money or paying off credit card balances.

b) Someone might have some wonderful personality traits, traits that would make that person a more desirable partner for anybody, compared with someone who lacked them. But those personality traits don't necessarily make that person a good match for *you*. Think of the first six items that are mentioned in the Boy Scout Law—which all of you Scouts out there remember, just as I do, years after your last merit badge. All together now: "Trustworthy, loyal, helpful, friendly, courteous, kind." A person who is all these things—and, to name just a few more, thoughtful, considerate, easygoing, and forgiving—would be a better partner for anyone than a person without these traits. But if that person had different standards for neatness from you, different attitudes and habits regarding money, different interests and tastes, different values and aspirations, and different attitudes regarding sexuality from you, then they would not be a good match for you, despite their (and your) wonderful personality qualities. There would be no basis for the two of you to affirm each other, and so love each other—as opposed to just being fond of each other because you're both such fine people.

c) With respect to some personality traits, it can actually be helpful if the two partners *don't* match up that well. (This is a point that is made in all the other books on marriage and relationships, and it makes me feel good to finally be able to agree with them on something.) If one partner is impulsive about buying things, and the other person is more cautious, they might have more conflict than a couple in which both partners are impulsive, but they'll probably turn out better in the end. Also, if your partner has personality strengths that you don't, you have the opportunity to develop those strengths by imitation. For example, Clyde was, as he described himself, "pessimistic by nature." This had always made it hard for him to persist in the face of frustration. Whether it was looking for lost keys or tracking down job leads, he would give up sooner rather than later. Clyde's wife, Maisie, was the opposite: an eternal optimist who never gave up. After being with Maisie for a while, Clyde noticed that almost all the time Maisie's persistence paid off, so he figured he'd try it himself. Whenever he'd get to the point where he was so frustrated he was about to give up, he'd ask himself, "What would Maisie do?" And he would do it, whatever it was (even though he didn't *feel* like doing it because he was so pessimistic), and sure enough, being persistent like Maisie paid off for him, too.

It's beneficial for partners to be different from each other—as they inevitably are, at least in some ways—as long as the differences are more the exception than the rule. But if the differences are the rule rather than the exception, there will be too much conflict and you won't be able to benefit from your personality differences.

d) Being on the same wavelength, which is key to having a sense of companionship and communion in marriage, is not exactly a matter of personality. It's more a matter of outlooks, beliefs, and attitudes. Two people can differ from each other in their personalities and yet be on the same wavelength. One of you might be cautious, detail-oriented, meticulous, and serious; the other of you could be reckless and impulsive, and not detail-oriented or meticulous at all. Yet you two see the world, and react to it, in much the same way. Your values are similar, your spiritual orientations are similar, your opinions on important social issues are similar, and the things that you are most devoted to in your lives are similar.

How you see the world, and how you react to it, cannot be reduced to a list of personality traits. Other factors determine what wavelength you're on: experiences you've had, influences from your family and other important people as you were growing up, books you've read, and a lot more. That's why two people can have similar personalities and yet not be on the same wavelength. And that's why two partners with quite different personalities can nevertheless be on the same wavelength.

8. But isn't it impossible to find someone of the opposite sex who is really similar to you, because men and women are so

different from each other that it's as if they were from different planets?

There's been a lot of this going around, stuff like:

Not only do men and women communicate differently but they think, feel, perceive, react, respond, love, need, and appreciate differently.[5]

I don't think so. Remember *Elvira Madigan*? Sue went to see it with a *guy* who loved it. So who's from what planet?

Which points up the first big problem with the different-planets notion: It stereotypes men and women. It just isn't the case that men, or even most men, are all one way with respect to how they think, feel, love, and so forth, and that women, as a group, are all some other way. The fact is that men differ *from each other* in all these ways, and the same goes for women. So, it's inaccurate and reckless to say that "men are this" and "women are that." Some of each group may be this, or that, but many others are not.

And while there is no doubt that men and women differ from each other in all sorts of ways, including some important ways, the notion that they are *so* different it's as if they are from different planets is greatly exaggerated. If you look at the scientific studies that have been done on the psychological differences between men and women in relationships, you will find that, while there are small to moderate average differences between men and women on some measures, they are swamped by the similarity between men and women on many other measures. And even in instances where *average* differences between the sexes are found, there is considerable overlap between the two groups. That is, because of the large individual differences among men as a group and among women as a group, you will find plenty of men who score more similarly to some women than they do to other men, and, likewise, women who score more similarly to some men than they do to other women. And the men and women who respond in these ways are not sissies or tomboys. They would be recognizable to you on the street as perfectly masculine men and perfectly feminine women.[6]

Even when substantial differences are found between men as a group and women as a group, we have to be careful to ask whether these are due to men and women being different from each other in some deep, essential way, or due to something else. For example, a number of studies have confirmed something many of us believe (and that may well be true): that, for women, sex is mostly about love and connection, while for men, sex is mostly about sex. But consider this study: The experimenter had men and women confederates approach strangers of the opposite sex and proposition them (yes, to go to the confederate's place to have sex). More men accepted the proposition than women did. And that shows that for men sex is about sex and for women it's about emotional investment and attachment, right? Not necessarily. Hey, big guy, do *you* ever worry about being beaten up and/or raped by a woman you meet at a bar or a party? She does. So the fact that more men than women accepted the proposition might well have been due to worries about safety that women (justifiably) have and men don't, rather than to some essential difference in how men and women feel about sex.

The research findings that cast the most serious doubt on the different-planets notion are those having to do with friendships between men and women. If the different-planets notion were true—if men and women really were so different in how they communicate, think, perceive, react, respond, love, et cetera—we would not expect men and women to relate to each other as friends. How could they be friends when there is no basis for mutual understanding? Yet the research shows not only that men do have close nonsexual friendships with women, but also that they experience more empathy and emotional intimacy in their friendships with women than in those with men, and that they report being *understood* more by women than by other men. Some men specifically seek out a woman to talk to, when they are in crisis, for these very reasons. All of these findings contradict the claim that men and women are so different that it's as though they were from different planets.[7]

Why, then, has the different-planets notion had such wide appeal? I think there are two reasons. First, there are plenty of obvious, *but superficial,* differences between men as a group and women as a group, and some of these differences do cause problems between individual men and women. Men spending entire weekends watching football is the most obvious example. Differences like this one make men and women *seem* more different from each other than they actually are.

The second, and more important, reason is this: Many individual men and women who married the wrong person soon enough come to experience how different they and their partner are from each other. They find it impossible to understand how their partner can think and emotionally respond so differently from how they do. And then the process of polarization that happens so often in unhappy couples only magnifies those differences: The more he talks about how important today's game is, the more she talks about how stupid and trivial football is. The partners find themselves completely mystified by each other (not to mention frustrated, irritated, and angered). So when someone comes along and says, "Hey, don't worry about it. Men and women are so different from each other, they're always ultimately mysterious to each other," that's a reassuring message. The couple can think, with relief, "It's not just us, it's everybody." There is a parallel here between the different-planets notion and the marriage-is-hard-work notion: They both give some comfort to unhappily married people. People in unhappy marriages might be able to ease their pain by thinking that men and women are from different planets. People in happy marriages know that we are all earthlings.

9. What if my partner and I are from different ethnic, racial, or religious groups? Does that mean we can't be similar enough on the compatibility dimensions to be a good match for each other?

No, not at all. There are many racially or religiously or ethnically mixed marriages where the partners are very compatible. The problems in these marriages generally come from outside the marriage: the prejudices of family-of-origin members, and the prejudices of society at large. These prejudices impose extra stress on the marriage and demand a higher level of coping from the partners than for partners who married within their social group. I think that too much has been made of religious, ethnic, and racial differences in marriage.

In fact, people can mistake the things they have in common as a result of their common ethnicity or religion for true compatibility. There is a certain familiarity that feels very comforting when you interact with someone who has the same origins as you, but that familiarity is based on superficial things, such as knowing about the same ethnic foods, understanding in-group jokes, and being able to use expressions from a foreign language. You two may be able to enjoy the understandings you have because of your common cultural origins. But that doesn't mean that you two will automatically have the same values, interests, reactions, or even spiritual outlooks. In fact, you two may have disagreements on things specifically having to do with the ethnicity or religion that you have in common.

Think about your very best friends. I wouldn't be surprised if at least one of them has ethnic or religious origins quite different from yours.

10. What about age differences?

I know of no evidence that age differences, in themselves, prevent people from being compatible. But my sense is that, beyond certain limits, they can be a problem. It's not just a matter of not being familiar with the same songs and TV shows, although that's certainly a part of it. Age differences can be a real problem if they are large enough to put the two partners at different life stages. The most common example, one I've seen over and over again, is when a woman in her thirties marries a man in his late forties or older. She wants a child and he doesn't—either because he feels he's too old ("Look, by the time the kid is eighteen, I'll be seventy") or because he's already had his own set of children. Another example is when a woman in her late thirties or early forties is very committed to her career, while her substantially older husband is disconnecting from the work world and moving into retirement. He wants to move somewhere warm where he can play golf every day, and he wants her to play with him. She doesn't want to play golf yet; she wants to work.

But there are exceptions. There's one couple I know in which the man is much older than the woman, and at a different life stage in at least a couple of ways, and they are wonderfully compatible. *What counts, in the end, is not the age difference itself, but the effects of the age difference on how close the partners are on the Three Dimensions of Compatibility.* (And as the first, and possibly the greatest, American psychologist, William James, once said, "A difference that makes no difference is no difference.") So the ball to keep your eye on is not the difference in your ages, but how compatible you are.

11. Is there only one right person for me?

No, there are many people out there who could be the right person for you. They all differ from each other in a variety of ways that would give your relationship with any one of them a flavor distinct from any of the others. One of them might be very into, say, stock-car racing; another might be into sailing. But if each of these people was very similar to you, overall, on the compatibility dimensions, each would be equally the right person for you. It would be very different, though, living with someone who was into stock-car racing than with someone who was a sailor. I think about people as if they were those many-faceted mirrored balls that reflect the light in nightclubs. Each one of us has many, many facets like that. And if someone matches us on some critical number of these facets, they can be right for us. But it doesn't necessarily have to be any particular combination of facets. It just has to be enough of them.

If you do marry one of these right people, and stay married for a long time (as you probably will), you may, at some point, meet one of those other right people—someone whom you could have married and been happy with too, if you had happened to meet him or her first. It's an uncanny experience. You say to yourself, "Gee, I could have married this person, and it would have been real different, but it still would have been great." You say this to yourself not with burning desire for that other right person, because you're happy with the person you did marry. But you can't avoid feeling a twinge of curiosity.

12. Isn't it hard to find one of these right people, like trying to find a needle in a haystack?

It's a little harder than marrying one of the many wrong people out there, but it's not that hard. People find the right person all the time, and they find them in the same places as they find the wrong person. That is, they find that right person among the people they happen to be thrown together with by chance: in their neighborhood, in school, in their office or other workplace, in their church. Or they meet in some truly chance way. I met Clark and Maggie when they were about sixty and had been happily married for thirty-five years. Marveling at how well matched they were, I asked them how they'd met. Maggie burst into laughter and replied, "He was on leave from his ship. [This was during World War II.] I was out with a couple of my girlfriends. It was a pickup in Times Square!" Another couple I know who are wonderfully well matched met on an airplane. He was on his way home from a funeral. What if his loved one had died a week earlier, or a week later? Or what if he'd been caught in a traffic jam, missed his flight, and had to take the next one? See what I mean about chance?

It's possible to find the right person almost anywhere, because you are *not* looking for some kind of one-in-a-million pattern of similarities. You are just looking for *enough total similarity on just Three Dimensions of Compatibility,* which could result from any of a variety of patterns.

It's amazing to think that wherever you happen to be you might find someone who is right for you, but that's how it happens. Sometimes people do find the right person through computerized dating services or carefully crafted singles ads. But often they just bump into the right person in the course of their everyday lives. My friend Freddy, after his divorce, placed singles ads, answered other people's ads, and went out with a dizzying number and variety of women. The woman he ended up marrying was his daughter's math tutor.

When we find the right person, it has a sense of inevitability to us, and that makes it hard to remember that our meeting came at the end of a long chain of events that went one way but could very well have gone another. It's weird when I think that if the 1956 Hungarian revolution hadn't happened, I would never have met Sue; or if her parents had decided to stay put instead of escaping, or had settled in Canada or Australia, I would never have met her. Sooner or later, though, with a little luck, I would have met one of the other right people for me. My life would have turned out to be very different from how it actually has—in ways I couldn't begin to imagine—but it would have been just as happy. So wherever you are, unless you are some kind of hermit, you have a good chance of meeting one of the many right people for you. Once you understand how to assess whether someone is one of those right people, the main thing you have to do is guard against marrying one of the wrong people—out of impatience, or desperation, or because of the pressure to get married—before one of the right people comes along.

■ PART TWO ■

Choosing
the
Right Person

7

AVOIDING BAD NEWS

I assume that the person you're thinking of marrying is a person of at least decent moral character and mental health. The ballpark of decent character and mental health is quite large, and almost all of us, even with all our flaws and hang-ups, fit into it. But not all of us. Some people have characteristics that would make them a bad match for anybody—they are *Bad News*.

To take an obvious example, men who are violent toward their partner are Bad News. No one should be married to a violent man but many women are. Either they didn't see the warning signs, or they chose to ignore them or misinterpret them. People can be enormously creative in finding ways to rationalize sticking with people who are Bad News.

Sometimes people rationalize in that way because it can feel great, a lot of the time, to be with a partner who's Bad News. Bad News people are often charming. More important, a Bad News partner can be very close to you on the compatibility dimensions despite being Bad News. The Bad News partner seems like a good match for you, and your love is real; if it weren't for the fact that this person is Bad News, you two could have had a great marriage. But Bad News, in its negative way, is like a royal flush in poker: It beats anything. If someone is Bad News, it doesn't matter how great it usually feels to be with them. *It doesn't even matter how compatible with you a Bad News person is.* This person is still someone whom you shouldn't marry—someone you shouldn't even be dating.

In this chapter I'm going to give you my sense of what it takes to really get to know someone so that you can find out if they're Bad News. Then I'll give you my own list of characteristics that qualify someone as Bad News.

Getting to Know Them

In order to be sure that someone isn't Bad News, you've got to really get to know that person—which inevitably takes time. Some people get married to a Bad News partner simply because they didn't know them long enough to encounter a situation in which their partner's true, Bad News colors came shining through.

Think about yourself for a moment: how long you've lived, all the different relationships you've had (romantic and nonromantic), all the good and bad things that happened to you as a child, all the different sides of you and of your life as you are right now, all the things about you that you're happy and proud about, all the things you're ashamed of and regret. That's a lot. It's a lot for your partner to get to know, and, naturally, there's every bit as much for you to know about your partner. It takes a lot of time for all that information to be exchanged and, often, specific but important bits of information won't come out unless they are prompted in some way—not because your partner is hiding them, but because those aspects of your partner need to be evoked by some specific event. For instance, someone may seem mellow, secure, and nonpossessive until you see them become enraged the first time you tell them you went out to lunch to talk business with a coworker of their sex.

A lot of the most important and objective information you get about people comes not from what they tell you, because that can be spun in many different ways, but from your direct observations of what they do. For example, someone can tell you how they relate to Mother, but you get much more information, possibly including some that your partner might not want you to have, by watching your partner and Mother interact.

To really get to know your partner, you need to spend enough time with your partner, in enough different situations, with enough of your partner's friends, associates, and family members, so that you get to know not only your partner but your partner's personal world.

When people lived in small, tight-knit communities, this was much easier then it is now: Everybody knew everybody else, people lived close to where they worked, and they married someone from within the community. Who the Bad News people were, or for that matter who the Bad News *families* were, was common knowledge. These days, people who meet in high school still can have a lot of background knowledge about their partner even before they start going out. They know each other's friends, maybe even their brothers and sisters; they may know people who have gone out with that person. People who meet in college know less about each other, up front, than people who meet in high school, but they still know quite a bit. People who meet on the job, after high school or college, know even less about each other, to start with, because they see each other only at work. People who meet at a singles bar or through a singles ad know nothing about each other, and it's easy to be fooled.

Because of how little we might know about people and their background when we first meet them, getting involved has become downright scary: Is that person really who they say they are? Getting romantically involved with a new person has come to feel so perilous that a private detective has written a book on how to get the lowdown on someone by searching through court and police records, bankruptcy records, and the like.[1] I would suggest to you that if you ever feel the need to do this kind of detective work on someone you're involved with, save yourself the trouble and just break up: You're getting bad vibes, and chances are your bad vibes indicate that the person is Bad News, even if you can't point to anything specific.

If you take the time to get to know your partner, and to get to know the people who make up your partner's world, and to observe your partner in action inside that world, you won't have to resort to detective work. You'll have enough information to know whether or not your partner is Bad News.

The Bad News Catalog

As a psychologist I try my best to be open-minded, understanding, and tolerant of negative characteristics in the people I meet, whether in my office or out of it. Accordingly, I have tried to keep this list short, restricting it to those characteristics of a person that I consider not just negative, but negative enough to qualify for definite exclusion.

Someone is Bad News if he or she:

* **ever was physically violent with you.**

This is in line with the policy of zero tolerance for physical violence in intimate relationships that is finally becoming accepted in our society. Your partner may have apologized after he was violent toward you, he may have promised never to do it again—but apologies and promises are all part of the pattern of violence. If your partner has already been violent with you before your marriage, you can bet that he will be violent with you, sooner or later, after he marries you and feels like he owns you. You may be wondering if people who are violent can learn to be nonviolent. The data are not encouraging. In a recent review of studies on the outcome of psychological treatments for violent men, the authors concluded that these violence-reduction programs are not very effective, and, because of that, "the very existence of such programs may actually increase the wife's risk, by leading to a false sense of security among battered women whose husbands have sought treatment."[2]

* **has been sexually unfaithful to you or to a previous partner.**

The parallel with violence is obvious. People don't change much in their basic nature, and the best predictor of anyone's future behavior is his or her past behavior. A partner who has violated your relationship in this way even before you're married will do it again—it's only a matter of time. And if your partner has cheated on someone else, chances are that you will be next, sooner or later.

* **lied to you once about something important, promised never to lie like that again, and then lied again.**
* **lied to you, and then tried to justify it by saying there was some kind of good reason to have lied to you.**

These two Bad News criteria are obviously related, but (to me, at least) the second is even worse than the first.

As children, we are taught that lying is wrong. Yet, as we get older, we receive many messages—and often we're hardly aware of them—that lying in our private, personal lives is not *that* wrong under certain circumstances. We may get into trouble if we don't watch out, but it's not that bad, especially if it looks like there's no alternative. That has been the message in many sitcoms, for example, from *I Love Lucy* to *Home Improvement*.

But let's think seriously about what lying really is. The philosopher Sissela Bok has pointed out that lying is a form of *coercion*.[3] Lying is like tying the other person's hands behind their back, because it prevents them from making the free choice that they would have if they had known the truth. Bok gives the example of a man who goes for his yearly physical, just before he is about to go off on his dream vacation. The results of the physical indicate to the doctor that the man has only a year to live. The doctor, thinking he is being kind to his patient, tells him that he's fine so that he can go on his dream vacation before he dies. But maybe if the man knew he was dying, he might have decided not to take the vacation and instead done something much more important to him.

Now let's consider two more examples, first someone who lied, promised not to lie again, and then did lie again. Bryce and Yolanda were in the early stage of their relationship, very much in love, and still getting to know each other. One day Yolanda was at Bryce's apartment and happened to see a document that seemed to show that Bryce had some significant debt. She asked Bryce about it, and he got visibly anxious and flustered. He told her he did owe that money, but that he was paying it off. Several months later, after Yolanda and Bryce had moved in together, an envelope came for Bryce with "Final Notice" stamped on it in red. When Bryce came home, Yolanda asked him to open the envelope in front of her and tell her what it was about. Bryce looked terrified but he did as she asked. Sure enough, it was that same debt, only larger now because Bryce hadn't paid a penny on it in the months since he'd first revealed it to her. Bryce broke down and cried and confessed to Yolanda that he had no money to pay off the debt and didn't know what he was going to do about it, but that somehow he would find a way. Yolanda then asked Bryce if he had any other debts. He said he didn't. She asked him if he was sure. Still in tears, he assured her he didn't. Only a couple of weeks later, another, similar envelope arrived but with a different return address. Yolanda asked Bryce to open that one in front of her, and it turned out to be a notice on another substantial debt. Yolanda's trust was severely shaken, and she pulled out of the relationship—rightly, I think.

Bryce was not some evil psychopath. He was just a person who was made very anxious by telling an unpleasant truth to someone else—or to himself, for that matter. He felt awful about lying—guilty, ashamed—and he repeatedly promised himself he'd tell the truth next time. But, inevitably, when the time came, he panicked and lied again. Despite his good intentions, and his many other fine qualities, Bryce was Bad News, and it was in sorrow that Yolanda listened to her inner wisdom and left him.

Rhona was even worse news. She and John were both over thirty, successful business executives, and had just gotten engaged. John's family was preparing a big party for his grandmother's eighty-fifth birthday, and John very much wanted Rhona to come with him so he could intro-duce her to his grandmother. Rhona told him that, unfortunately, she had an important business trip to Boston on the very day of the party. John was terribly disappointed, but he knew from his own experience in busi-ness that trips like Rhona's couldn't be postponed, no matter what. He went to his grandmother's party by himself and made apologies for Rhona. A few days later, John was hanging up his coat in Rhona's front closet when he noticed a brightly colored lift ticket attached to Rhona's ski jacket. He looked at it and was shocked to discover that it was dated the day of his grandmother's party. When John confronted Rhona with the ticket she calmly responded that she had indeed been in Vermont, not Boston, skiing with a couple of her girlfriends. John asked her why she'd lied to him. Rhona replied, matter-of-factly, "If I'd told you I was really going skiing you'd have never let me do it."

Rhona felt she was perfectly justified in lying. People like Rhona— who feel that lying is OK if there is "good reason" to lie, and who don't feel guilty lying—are *extremely* Bad News. They are downright scary because they see nothing wrong in acting coercively toward the person they supposedly love, and they do it repeatedly.

Trust is the foundation of marriage. We all know that. Whether someone has lied to you cold-bloodedly or out of blind impulse, the result is the same: You can't trust them. You can't be married to them.

* seems to drink too much.

All of us tend to *underestimate* the drinking and the drinking-related problems of the people close to us. Consequently, if you've come to the point where you *think* that maybe your partner drinks too much, you can be quite sure that you're right. Unfortunately, once you've discovered that your partner drinks too much, there's nothing you can do about it. Only the person with the drinking problem can do something about it. And the only thing to do about it is to stop drinking.

If you tell your partner that you think they drink too much and they immediately quit drinking and stay alcohol free for a good long time (by which I mean at least one year), then OK, you can marry: Your partner is now a *recovering* alcoholic, not an active one. But, if, as is more likely, your partner denies having a drinking problem, or mumbles something about cutting down, then you have to cut your losses and get out of the relationship. There is nothing more heartbreaking and devastating than being married to an active alcoholic.

* uses illegal drugs at all, or abuses prescription drugs.

I don't think that this one needs any explanation, but I'll tell you a story: One of the most heartbreaking cases I've ever had was a couple in their early thirties in which the husband had a long history of drug abuse that had overshadowed their marriage from the very beginning. They had come to me, once the husband had stopped taking drugs, to help them heal the wounds caused by his many years of addiction. We met two or three times, and things seemed to be going well. Then I received a call from the wife. She told me that her husband had died—dropped dead in the living room, right in front of her. The autopsy revealed that his death had been caused by a drug overdose.

* has contempt for their opposite-sex parent.

I've seen this more in men than in women. If your partner has contempt for their opposite-sex parent, there is a good chance that he will not respect you, either.

In college, a new roommate came into the apartment I was sharing with a couple of other guys. I asked him what his father did. He said, "He's a surgeon." I asked him what his mother did. He said, "She's an idiot." I later learned from a woman who'd gone out with him for a short time that he was intensely Bad News. In general, it's a good sign if your partner likes their opposite-sex parent, and a bad sign if they don't.

* habitually makes fun of you, criticizes you, or otherwise humiliates you in front of others.

Your partner might say it was only meant as a joke. But as Redd Foxx (the star of *Sanford and Son*) used to say in his nightclub act, "Don't mind me folks, I'm only serious." A person who habitually makes fun of you, criticizes you, or otherwise humiliates you in front of others can't possibly respect you. Keep away.

* seems to want to control you in a number of small ways.

This is a person who always seems to be bossing you around, even on little things that are no concern of theirs: what toothpaste you should use, how you should wear your hair, what's the "right way" to slice an onion, or fold a napkin, or read the Sunday paper. And if you don't do these things the "right way," they get angry at you. I find people like this scary. If they want to control you on the little things, they'll also want to control you on the big things—on everything.

* gives you the feeling that they're Bad News.

The great composer and band leader Duke Ellington once was asked for his definition of good music. Duke said, "If it *sounds* good, it *is* good." Likewise, with people who are Bad News: A person who feels like Bad News *is* Bad News. It doesn't matter if you can't put your finger on exactly what it is that gives you that feeling, or if you can't put it into words. As I'll explain in the next chapter, we know a lot more than we can say. So if you get the feeling that someone is Bad News, listen to that feeling, take it seriously, and walk away.

One day I was talking with my friend Duncan about people who are Bad News, and he told me this story: "I went out once—and I mean just one time, a long time ago—with a woman who gave me the feeling that she was Bad News. She was pretty, and sexy, and interesting to talk with. But by the end of the evening I had a funny feeling about her. I couldn't say exactly what the feeling was. It wasn't that I felt spooked or even uncomfortable—it was quite pleasant spending the evening with her. It was just a funny feeling *about her*, a feeling that said to me, 'Don't call her again.' I didn't. But over the years that followed I was able to keep tabs on her, out of morbid curiosity, I guess, and see how her life developed. I'll spare you the gory details. All I'll say is that, on the surface, she was very successful, but along her path to success she left a lot of human wreckage: her first husband, for sure; her second husband, probably; even her mother, who was dying of cancer when this woman said something really devastating to her." Bad News.

YOU MAY BE having either or both of two reactions to this Bad News list. First, you might be thinking that it's too short. In particular, if you are a woman, you might be wondering why I didn't include men who never grew up, can't love, hate women, are commitment phobic, and so on. Well, if you're wondering about it, that means you already know that such men are Bad News. I certainly think they are. You've probably read some of the many books about these sorts of men. You should carefully consider what those books have to say. There may be other characteristics that, because of your own particular life experiences and hard knocks, would qualify a potential partner as Bad News for you. I certainly invite you to add those items to the list. (And, of course, each of us has some *unconscious* Bad News criteria that we use in disqualifying people as potential mates—without even being able to put those criteria into words. We just *feel,* as Duncan did, that a particular person is Bad News.)

The other reaction you might be having to my list is the opinion that it's too strict and unforgiving. You might be thinking, for example, "Someone hits you only once and then apologizes, but you should immediately blow him off instead of giving him another chance?" I admit that my Bad News criteria are very conservative—OK, they're strict and unforgiving. But with regard to behaviors as damaging as violence, drug taking, and infidelity, I think it's much better to err in the direction of safety than the other way. You can disagree with me and go ahead and marry a Bad News person anyway. It may even work out; anything is possible. But if it doesn't, don't say I didn't warn you.

The Bad News Disagreement

The Bad News characteristics I just listed make the people who have them a bad match for anyone. And you have your list of Bad News characteristics that make someone a bad match for you. In addition to these, there is one *issue* that, if the two partners don't agree on it, automatically makes them Bad News for each other. They should *not* marry each other if they disagree on it. That issue is:

Should we have children? Disagreement over whether to have children is a deal breaker because of how very important children are (by their presence or absence) in people's lives, and because people have to know, *way in advance,* what to expect. You cannot get married at twenty-five, and then wait to decide until you are thirty, because if you disagree at that point you'll be in a real pickle. (I am consistently amazed at how many reasonable and intelligent couples find themselves in it.) You have already invested a great deal of emotion in your relationship and formed a bond. As a result, the one of you who wants to have children has to go through the agony of deciding whether it's worth breaking this bond in order to have them. If you do decide to find a different partner, one who's willing to have children, you're starting over again rather late in the game. Especially if you're a woman, you'll feel that you don't have a lot of time. And then there is always the fear—and, unfortunately, the chance—that you won't find a suitable partner within the time you feel you have. In short, realizing that you disagree about children at the point in your marriage when one of you is ready to have them causes catastrophic turmoil.

So you have to agree in advance. If one of you wants to have kids, you cannot be satisfied with your partner's saying that kids *might* be OK. A partner who is not sure about having kids must promise, at the very least, to go along with it, if that's what you want. Likewise, if, before you get married, you both are unsure about having kids, making the marriage commitment can be only with the understanding that if somewhere down the line one of you decides you want them, the other will go along with that.

Once you've made your deal about kids, there can be no changing of minds.

You also must agree on a time frame within which to begin trying to conceive your first child—whether within two years of getting married, five years, ten years, et cetera. Sometimes people who initially agreed to have children will later say, "Now is not the right time," and continue saying it until it's too late to conceive. Whether these people can't admit to themselves that they don't want children, or know it but can't admit it to their partner, the result is the same. Agreeing in advance on a time frame for conception establishes that the "now is not the right time" argument is inadmissible.

Finally, you must decide in advance on *how many* kids, and stick to that agreement. Rudy was forty-seven and Sally was thirty-two at the time they came to see me. This was Sally's first marriage, Rudy's second. From his first marriage, Rudy had a twenty-five-year-old daughter who was about to get married herself. Rudy and Sally had one child of their own, a three-year-old son, Chip. Each partner told a different story about their original deal on number of children. Sally said that they had agreed on two. Rudy said they'd agreed on one definitely, with the understanding that two might be a possibility.

Sally came from a close and warm family where she got along wonderfully with her two sisters. For her, it was very important to give Chip the gift of a sibling. The way Rudy saw it was that he was forty-seven and already had two kids, and that he was now too old to have a third. Rudy and Sally spent many hours, in my office and out of it, communicating and negotiating about whether to have another child but were unable to come to agreement. Because of Sally's strong commitment to having more than one child, her grief over having only one was as intense as if she'd wanted children and had none at all.

While you must decide in advance on whether to have children, and how many, I think it's difficult to decide in advance about whether you would adopt if it turned out that you couldn't have children of your own. The experience of infertility is an emotional roller coaster that can change people's ideas about adoption any which way. If it's your bad luck to take that ride, you'll have to get off it and regain your balance before you can begin to decide if adopting is the right thing for you.

NOW THAT the Bad News is out of the way, we can get on with determining how compatible you and your partner are.

8

FEELING YOUR
COMPATIBILITY

Feelings and Decisions

We know more than we can put into words. The knowledge that we have but can't put into words is available to us through our feelings. Getting in touch with our feelings is the *only* way we can access that information. And it is often just that information that is most important to us for making the right decision—whether about something small, like which CD to buy, or something big, like which person to marry.

Imagine walking into a record store having vowed to yourself that you will buy only one CD. Not three CDs or even two—just one. But you find two: a Rolling Stones CD and a Beatles CD. So you stand there with the two CDs in your hands, trying to decide, weighing the pros and cons: "Well, I have six Beatles CDs and only four Stones CDs. But the Beatles CD has one song I've always wanted. But the Stones CD costs two dollars less than the Beatles CD. . . ." You go through that "rational" decision-making process, *but you still can't figure out which CD to buy.* So you flip a coin: Heads it's the Beatles, tails it's the Stones. It comes up heads—the Beatles. Suddenly, you get a funny feeling in the pit of your stomach. You put down the Beatles CD and you take the Stones CD to the checkout counter.

What just happened? The coin flip got you in touch with a feeling, and that feeling contained the information that enabled you to decide the Stones CD was the one you wanted more.

It's important to understand several things about feelings as information in decision making:

—A feeling is not purely mental, although it has a mental component. You experience a feeling, first of all, as a physical sensation in your body.

—The feeling may serve as information for you, even though you can't articulate the feeling in words, as in the CD example I just described. In that case, the feeling *is* the information.

—You may be able to unpack the feeling by attaching words to it. And if you can do that, then you can get even more information out of it. For example, if you had focused for a few moments on that gut feeling you got in the CD store, you might have eventually gotten to "The Stones are really my favorite group these days," or "I always feel better if I can spend under ten dollars for a CD than if I spend over ten dollars," or some other thought that was contained in the felt sense you got— thoughts that you wouldn't have found "rationally."

—Making a decision by relying on the information in your feelings is *not* irrational. There is no contradiction between basing your decision on the facts and relying on your feelings. Getting the facts and getting a felt sense are two sequential steps in making a fully informed decision. First you get the facts, and then you use them as the raw material for getting your felt sense.

You may be interested to know that "rational" decision making is actually impossible without input from your feelings. Neurobiologists have found that people with damage to the parts of their brain that process feelings can't make personal decisions (like which jacket to wear or which CD to buy) even though they can solve all sorts of impersonal problems, like puzzles and math problems. Their intelligence is intact, but they are stumped when making personal decisions because they don't have their feelings to guide them.

We all have the ability to listen to our feelings—to get a felt sense and then use that as a source of information. As you work through the next three chapters on the compatibility dimensions, I'm going to be asking you, from time to time, to focus on your feelings and get a felt sense of how compatible you and your partner are. When I ask you to do that, I would like you to get quiet, listen to your body, and become aware of the felt bodily sense that you're experiencing. That felt sense could be something quite specific and localized, like a funny feeling in the pit of your stomach. Or it could be something you just feel in your body as a whole—something much more subtle that's hard to describe in words. But you know it's there and you feel it. Once you get that felt sense, don't try to do anything about it. Just experience it.

What I've just described is the beginning of a technique called "focusing." Focusing helps people use their feelings in dealing with personal problems and in making decisions. An entire book, *Focusing,* has been written on it, but you don't have to read it to work through the next three chapters of this book.[1] By doing just the beginning of focusing— getting a felt sense—you will be getting important information from your feelings about how compatible you and your partner are. If you do read *Focusing,* it may help you get more information from your feelings, especially if you are working through this book by yourself.

What's most important for you to understand is that when I ask you to focus in on your feelings, I do *not* want you to talk to yourself, be analytical, or try to figure anything out. (Remember that in the CD example you got the most important information only after you stopped doing that.) All I want you to do is get quiet, listen to your body, and pay attention to the felt sense that your body produces.

The Hand-Rotation Exercise

Once you get that felt sense, I'm going to ask you to express it nonverbally, with your hands. You can try it right now. Here's how you do it:

1. Put your hands together so that they match up exactly, as if you were praying (see Figure 1).

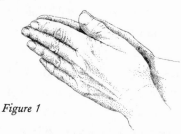

Figure 1

2. Choose one of the three compatibility dimensions—Sexual, Practical, Wavelength—to focus on. If you want to refresh your memory about the dimensions, turn back to chapter 2. (Don't try to do that with your teeth. Separate your hands for a moment.)
3. Now think of someone you know well. Not your current partner, someone else—a friend, a coworker, a relative, or someone you'd been romantically involved with in the past.
4. Try to get a felt sense of how compatible you and that person are on the dimension you've chosen. (Don't worry if at this point you don't have a clear and detailed understanding of what that dimension is about.) Play the mental video you have of that aspect of your relationship with that person. Visualize key incidents that seem to exemplify that dimension. As you do, pay attention to how your body feels. Again, don't talk to yourself, be analytical, or try to figure anything out. Just listen to your body and get a felt sense of you and that person on that dimension. Get the feeling of all of that as a whole.
5. Now, keeping your hands together, rotate them with respect to each other until it *feels* like the angle between your hands matches your felt sense of how alike or different you two are on that dimension. For example, you might rotate your hands just a little (Figure 2)—you feel very close to that person, very compatible, on that dimension. Or

you might rotate your hands so that they are pointing in very different directions (Figure 3)—you feel far apart from that person, not very compatible, on that dimension.

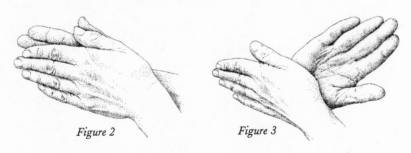

Figure 2   *Figure 3*

Your options in rotating your hands range from rotating them 180 degrees so that they point in opposite directions to not rotating them at all. You will know when you've rotated your hands the right amount—you'll feel that in your body too.

OVER THE COURSE of the next three chapters, from time to time, I'll be presenting you with what I call *defining questions*. Some of these defining questions will be followed by this icon:

The hand icon means that I would like you to do the Hand-Rotation Exercise for that defining question. For other defining questions there is no hand icon, but I certainly invite you to do the Hand-Rotation Exercise for any of them, if you feel it would be helpful.

If you are working through this book with your partner, together you can unpack the information in your feelings through the process of dialogue that I will be asking you to go through at the end of each of the next three chapters. But the first step in that dialogue is for each of you to be able to get a felt sense of your compatibility and then express that felt sense, to yourself and your partner, using the Hand-Rotation Exercise.

9

THE PRACTICAL DIMENSION

The Major Tasks of Day-to-Day Life

Once you marry and begin to coordinate your lives together, the list of things for you to agree on or disagree on becomes endless. The items on that endless list range from small ones such as "What should we have for dinner tonight?" and "Who's cleaning up after dinner tonight?" to medium ones such as "Should we buy that megascreen TV now while it's on sale or later when we actually have the money to pay for it?" to big ones such as "Should we chance our life savings on that business venture that looks so promising to you?" or "Should we invite your mother to live with us, now that she's a widow?"

The various issues you and your partner must decide on differ from one another in their *scale,* that is, in how much time, effort, and resources they will require. And they differ from one another in how frequently they come up and how predictable they are—whether they come up every day and are very predictable (dinner), or every once in a while and are moderately predictable (the TV), or very rarely and unpredictably (the business opportunity). But no matter how routine and predictable the issues are, *none of them is without importance.* Couples sometimes make the mistake of thinking that the "little" things they argue about are not important. They forget that the little things are what our lives are made of. When you're hungry, what you're having for dinner *is* important. And when you're tired, who's cleaning up after dinner *is* important. And if you don't agree about enough of these little, everyday things, you can't maintain the sense of mutual caring that is so important for lasting love.

For example, imagine that you and your partner both come home tired from work one evening. You say, "I'm too tired to cook. Let's eat out," and your partner says, "It's too expensive to eat out as much as we do. Let's eat in." You're likely to think that your partner doesn't care about how tired you are, especially if you're the one who usually does the cooking, and your partner is likely to think that you don't care about their money worries.

With such a great number and variety of things to agree or disagree about in your day-to-day life, how on earth do you go about figuring out how compatible you are? The first step is to see that all the items on that endless list involve things that have to get done—*tasks*. When I say tasks, I don't only mean chores like taking out the garbage. I mean everything. Having fun on Saturday night, for example, is a task because if you don't *do* something—go out, stay home and play cards—you won't have fun on Saturday night.

Once we recognize that all the items on the Practical Dimension involve tasks, we can make sense of them by grouping them together into the major tasks of day-to-day life. Those major tasks are the main things that you, as a couple, have to get done—day in, day out, week in, week out—to keep your life running smoothly. What couples have to do in their marriages, day to day, can be categorized into five major tasks:

1. Making Money
2. Spending Money
3. Maintaining Your Household
4. Filling Your Free Time
5. Dealing with Your Families

Each of these tasks blends into some of the others in a variety of ways. For example, how we fill our free time involves how we spend money, and it can also involve how we deal with our families.

Most important, how any couple handles these tasks always has something to do with how the partners feel about *gender roles—that is, about how* labor *and* power *are divided, given that one partner is a woman and the other partner is a man.* The gender roles that you think are proper in marriage constitute your *model of marriage,* the model you will try to follow in your own marriage. Because the model of marriage you choose will have an important influence on how you and your partner handle the major tasks of day-to-day life, let's look at the models you can pick from.

Models of Marriage: You Pick One

When it comes to buying a car, there are so many models to choose from it can be confusing. It isn't confusing to pick your model of marriage: There are only three. We can call those models *traditional marriage, equal marriage,* and *nontraditional marriage.*[1]

Traditional Marriage

This is the model of marriage that you see in many old sitcoms, from *Leave It to Beaver* to *Father Knows Best.* It is the model of marriage that many members of the postwar, Baby Boom generation grew up in, and that some of you who came along even a generation or more later also grew up in.

In a traditional marriage there is a big difference in power between the husband and wife. That is because money is power, and in a traditional marriage the husband earns all the money. The basic deal in traditional marriage is that the husband is responsible for making all the money and the wife is responsible for doing all the housework, including everything involved in taking care of the kids. The wife might work full-time outside the home until the first child comes along. But the understanding is that her job is much less important than her husband's. She'll quit her job soon after she becomes pregnant and she won't go back to work again until the children are grown, or maybe ever. Meanwhile, for as long as she is working she will still be expected to do the lion's share of the housework, because that's what's expected in traditional marriage. This burden of housework on top of a full-time job has been called "the second shift."[2] Around the house, the husband is responsible for the few things that are considered "men's work": taking care of the yard, maintaining the cars, doing home repairs, et cetera. He might "help" with some household chores, but he's not expected to help routinely.

Because the husband makes all the money (or, if his wife is working, because his role as income earner is considered more important than hers), he typically has more say over how the money is spent. Very big decisions about what to buy—like which house to buy—may be made jointly, but how to finance those purchases will generally be decided by him. Likewise, decisions about how much credit card debt to carry are made by him, and his wife will have to answer to him if she exceeds the limit. Meanwhile, he has more freedom to buy the things that he wants. After all, he earned the money. So if he wants to buy that very expensive camera or rod and reel, he'll go ahead and do it. His wife might complain about it, but she can't stop him. It's his money.

Because it's his money, the husband will have the lion's share of the authority over how much of it is saved and where the savings are put. The wife might not even know how much is being saved or where it is.

Who takes care of the monthly bills in a traditional marriage is a toss-up. If they're considered part of the housework, she'll do them; if they're considered part of the *finances,* he'll do them.

The power difference between husbands and wives in traditional marriage also has implications for the last two tasks, Filling Your Free Time and Dealing With Your Families. For example, if the husband wants to spend every Saturday playing golf with his buddies, he can probably do it because, after all, he works so hard supporting the family Monday through Friday. Likewise, if a situation comes up where someone in his family or the wife's family needs some kind of significant help, especially financial help, the husband in a traditional marriage may well have more say in whether that help is given.

Some of you may find my description of traditional marriage a bit negative. I don't mean it that way. Traditional marriage has worked for many couples over many generations, and it still does. It has two distinct advantages over the other models. First, there is a clear definition of roles. There's no question about who's responsible for what, and so there is no need for ongoing negotiation. In the other models, who does what is much less clearly defined and often in need of last-minute negotiation. The second advantage of traditional marriage is that there is no uncertainty about child care. The wife takes care of the kids, and the couple don't have to seek out relatives, baby-sitters, nannies, or day care centers to take care of them. Traditional marriage can be gratifying for both partners, as long as they agree on having that model. Within the general model of traditional marriage that I've described (and in the other two models as well) no two marriages are exactly alike. Each couple creates their own, individual, traditional marriage. They arrange their lives in their own unique way so that the model will work for them.

Equal Marriage

Equal marriage is not exactly the opposite of traditional marriage, but it's very different. Both partners work outside the home and are expected to even if there are kids. The husband's job and the wife's job are considered equally important even if one of them earns a lot more than the other.

In equal marriages all the money is considered to be "our money." The partners have equal authority and control over it—again, even if one partner earns a lot more than the other. The partners may have separate checking accounts, and from one month to the other either one may be contributing more of the money to cover expenses. Who pays more doesn't make a difference, though, because all the money is "our money." How much is spent out of whose checking account is just a bookkeeping technicality.

Decisions about what big items to buy, how much to pay for them, and how to pay are mutual decisions, with the husband and the wife having equal power in making them. Likewise, decisions on how much debt to carry are mutual decisions. They are both free to buy little things like dress patterns or CDs for themselves but neither would buy even a medium thing, like a sewing machine or CD player, without running it by the other partner first. (In these situations, the partner will generally say something like "Sure. You didn't really need to ask me," and mean it, but will be grateful to have been consulted anyway.) As in traditional marriage, bill paying is a toss-up. Sometimes it's divided up, sometimes one of the partners does it all. Saving money is a semi-toss-up: How much of the money to save is generally decided upon jointly, but who is in charge of *how* to save it varies. In some equal marriages both partners decide where to put their money. In others, one of the partners is identified as the financial wizard and decides on how to save but keeps the other partner informed. Everyone knows where the money is.

Housework is shared in equal marriages. It can be divided in any way, and how it's divided can change and evolve over time. But whichever way it's split, neither partner feels as if one is doing more than the other. (In many equal marriages what the partners do to divide the housework is this: Each one picks the things that he or she least minds doing—it's good if the two partners *do* differ in this one way—and for the things that are left over they alternate.) Often there is conflict when one partner's standards for performing a housework task are not as high as the other's.

When kids come along, neither partner automatically gets the role of primary caretaker. Since neither partner's job is considered more important, each of the partners is expected to make whatever changes are necessary in work schedules and work commitments to accommodate the baby—which can often be very tricky. Even in well-established equal marriages, it can be tough for the partners to decide how, and how much, each is going to cut back on work so they can take equal responsibility for the baby. Most often, they have to find someone they can trust to take care of the baby while they're both working. (Of course, all couples in marriages where both partners must work face that same problem, whether they are in an equal marriage or not.)

Even if the couple does employ someone to care for the child while the partners are at work, the husband in an equal marriage is much more involved in child care than a traditional husband is. In equal marriage, it's not just that the husband does more of the child-care *work* than in traditional marriage; he not only executes many of the tasks involved in child care but also is *responsible for planning them, keeping track of them, and making sure they get done*. For example, he not only takes the kids to the doctor for their immunizations; he keeps track of when they have to get their shots and he schedules the appointments.

AN EQUAL MARRIGE: TORREY AND NELSON. Torrey and Nelson have had an equal relationship from the very start. Even before they got married they started to think of all their money as "our money" and merged their finances into one account. Their solution to division of housework was that they did a lot of it together: They divided up the housecleaning and did it all on Saturday mornings, so they spent identical amounts of time on it. Nelson describes himself as more "food oriented" than Torrey, who can skip a meal and not notice it when she's preoccupied with her work, so as a result he is the one who ended up taking responsibility for meal planning and shopping. But Torrey is the better cook, so she has done almost all the cooking. They are flexible about who cleans up after dinner, depending on who is less tired on a given night.

Torrey and Nelson have two children. Torrey took only a short maternity leave after each one before returning full-time to her job in commercial sales. From the beginning Torrey and Nelson have relied on live-in child-care help—including the occasional emergency grandmother. There have also been numerous occasions when, in the absence of a live-in or grandmother, one of them had to take full responsibility for the kids (and adjust their work schedule accordingly) when the other was away on a business trip.

THERE ARE advantages and disadvantages to equal marriage. One advantage is that neither partner is saddled with the full responsibility for anything. Another advantage is that with both partners working outside the home, in the public sphere, there is less of a chance that they will start to feel out of touch with each other because they have very different lives. The obvious advantage for the woman is that she is economically empowered and, as a consequence, is not dependent on her man.

The major disadvantage of equal marriage is the higher level of confusion and chaos than in traditional marriage, because the gender roles are not fixed. For example, if Johnny starts to vomit in school, who leaves work to pick him up? Well, that depends: Who has the emptier schedule that day? Who works closer to the school? Who has the kinder boss? Who picked Johnny up the last time he got sick in school?

Nontraditional Marriage

This is somewhere between equal marriage and traditional marriage. There is a lot of variation in the way couples set up their nontraditional marriages. Some nontraditional marriages are closer to traditional ones and some are closer to equal marriages.

In nontraditional marriages both partners work, and the wife may earn as much as the husband or even more. Both partners may be equally interested in and involved in their jobs. And decisions about how to spend and save money may be made in much the same way as they are in equal marriage.

The defining feature of nontraditional marriage is the attitude toward child care: The wife has the primary responsibility for that because both partners feel that it's best for children to be raised by their mothers, if that is financially possible. When the first baby comes along, it is the wife who makes the big changes in her work schedule to accommodate the baby. These changes range from reducing her working hours at her present job, if that's possible, to changing to a less demanding job, to quitting work entirely for a few years—maybe until all the kids are in school.

Even if the wife remains at work during the children's preschool years, she is still considered to be the one who is primarily responsible for them. The husband may help in doing what needs to be done, but it's the wife who has the burden of worrying about how and when these things will be done. So, for example, Daddy might take the kids to the doctor for their shots at the start of the school year. But it was Mommy who remembered that the kids needed those shots and who set up the appointment. If little Johnny pukes in school, it's generally Mommy who leaves work to pick him up.

Likewise, the husband might help with housework, maybe even a lot, but in many nontraditional couples that help is mostly with the execution rather than with the planning. He may go out to buy the groceries, but it is his wife who plans the meals, compiles the shopping list, and tells him that if he doesn't go to the supermarket right now they're not going to eat dinner tonight.

In a nontraditional marriage, a wife who bears most of the responsibility for making sure that the housework gets done can feel as if she's working a second shift even though she is not physically doing all the work herself. On the other hand, she generally does have more power in financial decision making than the wife in a traditional marriage.

TWO NONTRADITIONAL MARRIAGES. The range of possibilities within the broad category of nontraditional marriage is illustrated by the marriage of Clay and Fredericka compared with that of Millicent and Lance.

The nontraditional marriage that Clay and Fredericka created is quite close to an equal marriage. Clay is an accountant and Fredericka is a software developer in a small high-tech company. After their daughter, Brittany, was born Fredericka took a one-year maternity leave, which was the longest she could take without losing her job. At the end of the leave, she arranged part-time child care for her daughter and returned to work— part-time, and with a telecommuting arrangement for a quarter of that time. This combination of adjustments allowed her to get home by midafternoon to be with Brittany. Clay made no adjustment in his work schedule, but he continued in his usual role as the food shopper and assumed responsibility for the laundry, which had been Fredericka's job up to that point. Clay and Fredericka continued to divide the rest of the housework pretty equally. Fredericka resumed full-time work when Brittany entered middle school, but she continued to have the flexibility of telecommuting part of the time. This allowed her to continue to be the one who supervised Brittany's homework, networked with other parents, and made sure that Brittany got to her various extracurricular activities .

Millicent is a nurse, Lance is a telephone lineman, and their nontraditional marriage is much closer to the traditional end of the spectrum. Millicent enjoys being a nurse, and her identity as a nurse is important to her sense of self, but she couldn't imagine anyone else taking care of her baby. So when the first of her two sons (spaced less than two years apart) was born, she stopped working; it wasn't until the younger son was three that she started working again. Lance supported Millicent's desire to stay home with the boys, and he took on as much overtime as he could during this period to make up for Millicent's lost income. Millicent had always done more of the housework, and after the boys arrived she did even more, especially since Lance was working all that overtime. When Millicent went back to work she did it very gradualy—literally a day at a time—as a contract nurse. At first she worked on Saturdays or Sundays and Lance would take care of the boys. Once the boys were in school, Millicent added a couple of weekdays to her work schedule, always working day shift so she could get back home at about the same time they did. When the boys were away at their grandparents' farm during the summer and holiday breaks, Millicent would work more, especially if she and Lance felt a pressing need for extra money, but she never went back to work full-time, and she always did most of the housework.

NONTRADITIONAL marriage works for couples who want a more equal power balance than in traditional marriage, but who also want to preserve the traditional role of the mother as the major caretaker for the children. And it works for couples who want more traditional gender roles, but not the complete separation of roles characteristic of traditional marriage.

It doesn't work when one or both of the partners would really prefer the traditional model, but they need two incomes in order to survive. This kind of situation can breed all sorts of frustrations and resentments. The wife would rather stay home, but she's got to work to support the household. The husband feels bad about not being able to be the sole provider, and he may feel threatened by the power his wife gains in the relationship because she's making money. (Remember: Money is power.) Meanwhile, the wife is expected to take care of the housework even though she's working full-time, and her husband is expected to help little if at all. But the wife needs a lot more help than that, so she asks for it. The husband resents her for asking him to do housework because that wasn't part of the deal when they got married; she resents him for pointing to that deal, since his side of the deal had been that he would do all the providing. They get angry at each other for not being able to have the kind of family structure they may have grown up in, or seen on television, but it's not their fault. It's just that the cost of living has increased much more, over the past couple of decades, than most people's incomes have, with the result that most families need two incomes to maintain the standard of living that required only one income in the first three decades after World War II.[3]

Nontraditional marriage also doesn't work when one of the partners thought that the plan was for an equal marriage. It comes about like this: She says she wants an equal marriage and he says he wants an equal marriage too. But what he means by "equal" is actually a nontraditional marriage, in which he will "help" but not be fully responsible for half the child care and housework. Whether intentionally or not, he has pulled a bait and switch on his partner. The clear implication for you and your partner is that if you are telling each other that you want an equal marriage, make sure you both mean the same thing by that—right down to who is responsible for what, and who does what for how many hours a week.

The Models of Marriage Rule

You and your partner may both already have an explicit agreement on the model of marriage you intend to follow. You've got to have one before you get married—before you get engaged, even. Too many important daily decisions about living your married life are determined by your model of marriage for you to get married without an explicit agreement about it. You would be amazed at the number of couples who haven't discussed their preferred model of marriage and get married without an explicit agreement on it, and the number of couples who think they've agreed on their model of marriage but haven't. In either case, the lack of explicit agreement about the model of marriage can cause enormous conflict—to the point of making the marriage unworkable. I feel so strongly about the importance of agreement on the model of marriage that I'm going to state it as a rule:

The Models of Marriage Rule
Marry only somebody who wants the same model of marriage as you do.

Remember that the descriptions I've given of the three models are only rough outlines, and that there is a lot of variation in how couples arrange their lives within each model. You and your partner will fashion your own personal version of the model you choose—and that version will work for you. But you have to agree on the model first. So if you haven't yet talked explicitly with each other about models of marriage, *start talking about it right now*. Ready or not, though, it's time for the Practical Dimension's first, and maybe most important, defining question.

—How closely do you and your partner match up on the model of marriage you want to follow?

Your model of marriage determines a lot about how you and your partner live day to day. It determines almost everything about the first major task of day-to-day life, Making Money.

How you and your partner accomplish the other tasks will depend on your model of marriage but more largely on your personalities. (This is the part of the book where you get to see if your personalities match up.) We'll start with the second major task, Spending Money.

Spending Money

As you've probably heard, money is the number-one fight topic in marriage. In fact, research has shown that couples fight more about money than about anything else. You may be thinking, Of course people fight a lot about money—who ever has enough money so that it's not a problem? I agree. Many couples simply don't have enough money to pay for what they need. And whenever anything is scarce—money included—there's conflict over it. What's interesting, though, is that even couples with plenty of money have terrible fights over it. Couples worth *millions of dollars* have had terrible fights about money, right in front of me, during marital therapy sessions.

Couples fight about money because they disagree about what to do with whatever money they have, whether that's a lot or a little. Specifically, their fights are over one or more of the five aspects of handling money that we're about to look at:

1. Spending priorities
2. Spending style
3. Savings orientation
4. Debt tolerance
5. Risk tolerance

Spending Priorities

One major way that people differ from each other is in what they think is worth spending their money on. A common example has to do with cars. Some people insist on buying only new cars, even if they have to go into debt to do it. Other people think it's ridiculous to spend so much money on something that's going to lose half its value as soon as it's driven off the dealer's lot and will buy only used cars. Some people think it's important to save enough money so that their kids will be able to go to the expensive, private college of their choice. Other people think their kids will do just fine going to a much less expensive state school. Some people prefer to spend their hard-earned money on experiences like trips to foreign places rather than on material possessions like furniture, and others prefer the opposite. I know a couple who live in a rented apartment and are saving up for an around-the-world trip instead of a down payment on a house. Other couples would never indulge in such a trip until they had their own home and plenty of financial security.

Whenever couples disagree about spending priorities, there's conflict. And in those conflicts it's particularly easy for each partner to feel righteous. That's because no set of spending priorities is *objectively* better than any other. It's all a matter of opinion:

"What, another video?!"

"But it's one of our favorite movies—one of *your* favorite movies."

"But it's always in the video store. We can rent it anytime. How long will it be before we've watched it sixteen times? That's how many times we'd have to rent it before we paid as much as you've paid to buy it."

"But, honey, we'll have it *forever*."

They're both right.

Regina and Wilt each made six-figure salaries, so lack of money was not exactly their problem. But they had very different spending priorities. In particular, Wilt had a passion for expensive watches, which Regina didn't understand. The $6,000 Rolex she could accept, barely. But then there was the $20,000 Baume & Mercier, and after that the $30,000 Patek Philippe. It wasn't that she missed the money; she just couldn't understand how he could spend that much money for just a watch. Wilt tried to explain that these were not just watches, but handmade, precision time pieces—works of art—and that they would be heirlooms that their son would inherit and then pass on. Regina didn't find these arguments convincing. More important, because she couldn't understand Wilt's passion for acquiring watches, she couldn't respect him for it. What Regina and Wilt experienced around the watch issue was the opposite of mutual affirmation, and as a result it chipped away at their love for each other.

Our spending priorities reflect not just our spending habits and our personalities. They reflect our *values*. Every time we make a decision on spending priorities, we are making a statement about our values—about what we think is more important than what and about what kind of life we think is worth living. When you and your partner agree on spending priorities, you are affirming not just each other's spending habits but each other's values. When you don't agree on spending priorities you are signaling that you disapprove of each other's values. And that mutual disapproval can powerfully undermine love.[4]

It's time, now, for you to think about how closely you and your partner agree on spending priorities. Think of purchases you've made together and purchases that you've seen your partner make. Think about your partner's most prized possessions; think of your own. Think of any discussions—or arguments—you've had about spending priorities. Think of all that, then focus in and get a felt sense of it.

> **—How closely do you and your partner agree on spending priorities?**
> **—Is there anything about your partner's spending priorities that puzzles or bothers you?**

Spending Style

By "spending style" I mean two related but distinct characteristics of how you go about buying things:

a) How *value oriented* versus *quality oriented* you are.

b) How *deliberative* versus *nondeliberative* you are.

Value-oriented shoppers don't want to pay full price. They don't just go into Bloomingdale's and buy that suit. They see if they can buy it cheaper somewhere else. If they can't find it cheaper somewhere else, they wait until Bloomingdale's puts it on sale. And if Bloomingdale's doesn't put it on sale, then they look around until they find something they consider "almost as good" that costs a lot less.

Quality-oriented shoppers, by contrast, are less concerned with getting the best buy than with getting the very best item, even if they have to pay a premium for it. If they don't have a lot of money, they will economize on things they don't consider important so that they have the money to buy the highest-quality versions of the things they do consider important. One woman told me that there were periods in her life when she ate nothing but beans or cold cereal for dinner so that she could buy the expensive, high-quality business suits that she deemed important. Quality-oriented shoppers will, naturally, look for a good price, but they will never compromise quality for price.

Shoppers who are deliberative about their purchases do a lot of research before they buy something. A deliberative shopper looking for a toaster will not just buy one because it's a good brand, has the features she's looking for, and is being sold at a good price. She will look at all the toasters on display, see what features they have and what they're selling for. And she will go to more than one store to make sure she's seen all the makes and models of toaster that are out there. She might even look at *Consumer Reports* and other such sources of information. In short, deliberative shoppers use an *optimizing* strategy for everything. Nondeliberative shoppers use a *satisficing* strategy. They don't see the point in going to all the time and trouble to research every purchase they make. If their toaster dies, they buy another toaster, and that's that. If the new one is a lot better than the old one, they're pleased—but all they were looking for was a toaster that works.

If you and your partner are very similar in your spending styles, then there's no problem. If you differ a bit in your spending styles, that could actually be an advantage, especially if you differ on how deliberative you are. The more deliberative one can put the brakes on when the other wants to make an unwise purchase. And the more nondeliberative one can teach the other partner that it's OK sometimes to just buy something. But if you're very different in your spending styles—and especially if one of you has a value orientation and the other has a quality orientation—there can be problems. The value-oriented one will think of the quality-oriented one as snobbish or self-indulgent. And the quality-oriented one will be irritated with the value-oriented one for buying "junk," or for going to great lengths simply to get a good buy.

Bud and Loretta are an example of this last type of conflict. They each make substantial salaries, so they don't have to worry about paying full price for medium-sized purchases such as hiking boots. They both have a strong quality orientation, but Bud also has a *very* strong value orientation.

One day, Bud, Loretta, and their toddler were at a store that sold hiking and camping equipment to buy Bud a high-end pair of hiking boots he wanted. It was a Saturday morning in May, so the store was crowded. Bud tried on the boots. They fit perfectly and looked great. He and the salesperson, a soft-spoken college student, took the boots up to the checkout counter, and just before they were rung up Bud produced a sale flyer that he'd found while doing spring cleaning. The flyer was from January and showed that at that time the store had been offering the boots for 30 percent less than their current price. Bud showed the flyer to the salesperson and demanded that the store sell him the boots for the January sale price. The salesperson politely explained that the sale price was no longer applicable. Calmly, quietly, but relentlessly, Bud continued to insist on the sale price and finally demanded to speak to the manager. (Meanwhile, although Bud's negotiation—as he called it—with the salesperson was being conducted in hushed tones, the people in the ever-lengthening checkout line behind Bud couldn't help but notice that something was going on.) The manager arrived, and she also politely but firmly explained that the boots were no longer on sale. Finally, without another word, Bud tossed his credit card on the counter and paid full price for the boots.

Loretta was mortified. Once she and Bud had left the store, she told him how embarrassed she was to be standing there next to him while he was being so "inappropriate," giving that salesperson so much grief. Bud replied that he was not inappropriate at all, and that he saw nothing wrong in trying to get the best price he could.

Bud and Loretta don't understand each other on the matter of value orientation. She might well interpret his behavior as stingy, mean, and rude. He might well interpret her reaction to his behavior as harshly critical, mean, and uptight. It's hard for them to respect each other when they interpret each other in these ways.

There would have been no problem, of course, if Loretta had the same extreme value orientation as Bud—if she'd been Laszlo, for example. Laszlo's wife, Vera, has enormous moxie. During World War II she survived on false papers, and she participated in a number of clandestine, and dangerous, anti-Nazi activities. (Laszlo has his own kind of strength, a quiet strength that enabled him to survive brutal slave labor during the war.) Nothing fazes Vera, certainly not shopkeepers. Whenever she has the chance she does exactly what Bud did because she shares Bud's extreme value orientation. Laszlo shares it too. He could never get himself to haggle as Vera does, but he loves it when she does it. He looks on and beams with approval.

At this point in your relationship you may not have a clear sense of your partner's spending style. For that matter, you may not have a clear sense of your own. You may not have thought about your spending habits in these terms before. If that's the case, you've got to be clear about your own spending style first. Please bear in mind that your spending style is not a matter of either/or, it's a matter of degree. You can be somewhere in between purely deliberative and wildly nondeliberative. You can be both value oriented and quality oriented, but more one than the other. Once you're clear about your own spending style, think back to all the experiences of buying things that you and your partner have shared. Those can include both instances where you bought something together and also instances where one of you bought something for yourself and the other just watched. Recall how in sync you and your partner seemed to be in, how you went about those purchases, how comfortable you felt. Putting all those experiences together, get a felt sense.

**—How similar are you and your partner in your
spending styles?
—Is there anything about your partner's spending
style that irritates you or causes you concern?**

Savings Orientation

This one is simple and straightforward and doesn't need much explanation: How much of a saver are you? People vary greatly on this, as on everything else. Some people save to the max; some don't save at all. For example, when a company has one of those plans where it will match, dollar for dollar, every dollar that the employee saves (up to, say, 15 percent of the employee's salary), some employees will save the entire 15 percent and won't understand why anyone wouldn't take advantage of such a lucrative deal. Other employees with the same income and overall expenses will put less into the plan or nothing at all. Your savings orientation has to do not only with how much you want to save, but with how good you actually are at saving. Some people keep promising themselves that they'll start saving right away—starting with the next paycheck . . . if they can. Other people don't do anything with their paycheck until they've put part of it away in savings first.

I'm not saying that you or anyone else *should* save; I'm a psychologist, not a financial planner. But you and your partner have to be similar in your savings orientation. To the degree that you are not, there will be conflict. The one who is less of the saver will be angry at the other for putting so much in savings when there are so many things they need *right now*. The saver will be angry because the other wants to fritter away money that they need for their future.

The older you are, the better idea you have of your own savings orientation. You've already established some track record of saving or not saving. But even if you're young, you can get some sense of your savings orientation. And you can get a sense of your partner's savings orientation by talking with each other about it.

**—How similar are you and your partner in your
savings orientation?**

Debt Tolerance

You may not have very much experience with saving yet, but chances are you do have some experience with debt. Just about everybody does: a car note, college loans, or credit card balances. And your debts, no matter how large or small they are, may bother you a lot, somewhat, just a little, or not at all. How tolerant you are of debt is the result of several interacting factors: your anxiety tolerance in general, the attitudes toward debt that you learned from your parents, the positive and negative consequences of debt that your parents experienced as you were growing up, and your own experiences with debt so far.

Partners have to be really close on this one—unlike, for example, spending style, where small differences between the partners can balance out and be beneficial. Even small increases in debt that go over the less tolerant one's limit will make that partner *very, very nervous,* and conflict will inevitably result. If the partners differ a lot in their debt tolerance, the less tolerant one will spend a lot of time being terrified—terrified and angry.

Julie and Stan were such a couple. Julie's parents were high school teachers with four kids. They weren't poor but they lived frugally, which happened to be right in line with their religious values. Stan's father owned a small chain of camera stores and was well-to-do. When I met them, Julie and Stan were graduate students getting by on very modest stipends. But armed with his battery of credit cards, Stan was able to get them anything he thought they needed. Stan was not exactly a shopaholic, but he did feel they needed more stuff than Julie did. What Julie needed most was not to be in debt. Even though Stan tried to reassure her that they had nothing to worry about as long as he paid at least the minimum every month, Julie worried. She was haunted by the specter of being in hock to the credit card companies forever, and she couldn't shake it.

These partners were really puzzled by each other, and each truly felt as if the other partner were from a different planet. But that wasn't because they were of different sexes. It was simply because they had different levels of debt tolerance. A few years after I met them, Julie and Stan got divorced. Conflict over debt wasn't the chief reason, but it was a factor.

You know how you feel about the debts you have. You know how you feel when you hear stories about people with huge debt burdens. You may have a clear sense of your partner's debt tolerance. If you don't, you can get one by talking about it. Once you've had that talk, focus in and get a felt sense.

—How similar are you and your partner in your debt tolerance?

Risk Tolerance

This one is also simple and straightforward. Every so often in life, opportunities come up that involve risk. And most often the risk is financial: buying that run-down house in an up-and-coming, "edge" neighborhood; quitting a secure job and taking a pay cut to work in a start-up company that has great potential but hasn't yet turned a profit; investing in somebody else's start-up business; or starting a business yourself.

If you and your partner are both risk takers, you'll be OK. If the risk you take pays off, you'll congratulate yourselves on how clever you both were. If it flops, you'll commiserate and chalk it up to experience.

If you and your partner are a little different in your risk tolerance, that's OK too. It may even be an advantage, as it is in spending style. The one who is more risk tolerant can point out when the other is being too cautious and encourage him or her to take the plunge. Likewise, the more cautious one can put the brakes on before the other drives them both off a cliff.

But if you and your partner are more than a little bit different in your risk tolerance, there will be conflict. The risk-tolerant one will constantly feel thwarted, and the more cautious one will live in constant fear of what the other might get them into next. There is also the potential for enduring resentments—not only if a chance taken by the risk taker lands the couple into trouble, but also if a chance not taken because of the cautious one's reluctance turns out, in retrospect, to have been a chance the couple should have taken.

Even if you and your partner have never had to make a risky decision together, you still have a clear sense of your partner's risk tolerance. That trait is something that runs through a person's behavior in a wide variety of situations. And you certainly have a clear sense of your own level of risk tolerance.

—How similar are you and your partner in risk tolerance?

Now it's time to put it all together and get a felt sense of how compatible you and your partner are overall on the major task of Spending Money. Please don't try to come to some "average" of your focusings on its five separate aspects. Instead, try to focus in on Spending Money *as a whole,* as if you hadn't already focused on its aspects separately.

—How similar are you and your partner on the major task of Spending Money?

Maintaining Your Household

This task has just two components, but they are very important, and they have to be dealt with every single day. Those components are (a) maintaining your personal physical environment and (b) maintaining your physical, bodily selves.

Maintaining Your Personal Physical Environment
By "maintaining your personal physical environment," I mean (a) how neat and clean you keep it and (b) how carefully you take care of the things you own.

HOW NEAT AND CLEAN YOU KEEP IT. Every day you make countless decisions, most of them unconscious, about how neat and clean your place is: whether to hang your coat in the closet or throw it on a chair, whether to make the bed in the morning or leave it unmade, whether to

138 • SAM R. HAMBURG, PH.D.

wash that coffee cup right now or leave it in the sink. These decisions are unconscious; you don't experience them as decisions, simply because they have become habits. Your own habits have a sense of inevitability to you, but not necessarily to your partner. Of course you always hang up your coat as soon as you walk in the door, and of course your partner doesn't. You start finding out about these differences early in your relationship. Once you start living together these differences start making a difference.

My impression—I know of no hard scientific data on this—is that neatness/cleanness is one domain in which there is a systematic difference between men and women. I believe—you guessed it—that men have more of a tendency to be messy and dirty. There are exceptions, of course, and sometimes they are extreme: Every once in a while I meet up with a couple in which the man is a neat freak. (I don't know why some men are this way. I suspect it's less a passion for neatness than for control.) Men like this can be so obsessive that they can't tolerate a speck of lint on their white (naturally—what other color would you expect?) carpet, or a book that isn't lined up exactly with the edge of the coffee table. For this kind of man, even a woman who is in the 99th percentile of neatness won't be neat enough. The same goes for a woman who's a neat freak. No man, unless he's a neat freak too, will be neat enough.

When one partner is a neat freak, whether there are problems will depend on who's expected to keep the household up to the neat freak's standards. In traditional marriages, in which the wife is expected to be in charge of cleaning, there will be problems if her neat freak husband expects her to meet his extreme standards. She just can't do it. She will feel oppressed by his standards, and worse, there won't be much that she can do about it. If he says to her, "You're not doing a good enough job," it's hard for her to reply, "If you don't like how I'm doing it, do it yourself." That wasn't part of the deal when they got married. In those cases, getting rid of her husband might be the only way out from under his oppression. (I was once consulted by a young woman whose husband was a neat freak *and* demanded oral sex from her every day. She left him.)

In nontraditional marriage, where the husband is expected to help with the housework, it will be easier for the wife to tell her husband to pitch in if he wants the house to be as neat as he requires. And in an equal marriage, whether the neat freak is the man or the woman, it will be quite easy for the other partner to say, "Well, then, do it yourself," because both are equally responsible for how their house is kept.

From all this we can derive a rule:

The Neat Freak Rule

If you believe you are a neat freak (or don't believe it but have been told that you are by more than one other person), then either (a) marry another neat freak, or (b) expect that you will be the one who does the extra work to keep the house up to your standards.

It's only fair.

The opposite situation, in which one partner (usually the woman) is reasonably neat and the other (usually the man) is an utter slob is much trickier. It is especially difficult if the man is expecting the woman to do more of the housework, and therefore pick up after him. Most women regard that as unfair, and so do I.

Whether you are a man or a woman (and I know several men who are married to women who are slobs) and are contemplating marrying a slob, proceed with caution. No matter what your sex, and who's responsible for the housework, you risk spending the rest of your life picking up after your slovenly mate. This is not to say that you can't ask your partner to make *some* changes in their habits that would be very important to you— you should. With good faith your partner could make those changes, using the two-step process that people use when they succeed in changing their habits: Step 1. Awareness. Step 2. Brute force of will. (A simple example: You want to stop biting your nails. Step 1. Notice whenever you put your fingers in your mouth [awareness]. Step 2. Shove your hands in your pockets [brute force of will].)

If you are the slob (and if you are, you know you are) then first of all you must admit it and acknowledge that your slovenly habits pose a real and nontrivial problem for your partner. Then you must be honest with yourself and with your partner about how much you could change those habits. And then the two of you must discuss whether those changes will be sufficient to prevent chronic arguments about neatness from ruining your life together.

Finally, a word about bathroom habits. The cap left off the toothpaste tube, the empty toilet paper roll not replaced—they're the least of it. I'm talking about wet towels composting in corners, hairs in drains, splatters of creams and lotions all over the sink and vanity, suspicious splatters of other kinds on surfaces that make contact with the human body (I'm talking about you, big guy), and so on. How well do you think you can live with each other, bathroomwise?

I bet you want to be finished with this section. All right, focus in, and get a felt sense.

—How close are your standards and your partner's on neatness/cleanness?

HOW CAREFULLY YOU TAKE CARE OF THE THINGS YOU OWN. People vary widely in how carefully they treat their possessions. Some people change the oil in their car every three thousand miles, some don't. Some people handle their records and CDs by the edges, other people handle them as if they were Frisbees. Some people never leave their charcoal grill out in the rain, others do that all the time.

As long as we are living on our own, we can treat our own stuff any way we wish. And we may well continue to do that after we get married. (Sue couldn't care less how I handle my CDs, although I happen to be careful about them.) But once you get married, a lot of your property is owned by both of you. So if you have very different views on how to take care of the things you own jointly, there will be conflict. (Couples who fight over letting the dog on the living room couch—if I had a nickel for every one of them, I could retire.)

You know how careful you are about your possessions. And you probably have an idea of how careful your partner is. Focus in and get a felt sense.

—How similar are you and your partner in how carefully you take care of what you own?

Maintaining Your Physical Bodily Selves

We're talking the basics: eating and sleeping. Let's start with sleeping.

People vary greatly in their need for sleep. Most people need between eight and nine hours a night to feel well rested (which, as you may have noticed, most people don't get—at least not on weeknights). Other people sleep no more than four or five hours a night and feel perfectly alert and rested all the next day. Some people have been poor sleepers all their lives, while others have been deep sleepers. Some people are day people, getting up early, feeling tired early, and going to sleep early, and some are night people, who do the opposite.

These differences in sleep needs and patterning are mostly hereditary in origin. There's not much that any of us can do to change how we sleep, or how much, without starting to feel bad as a result. That means that if you and your partner are very different on sleep, you can't come to some kind of compromise (such as "Instead of you going to sleep at eight and me going to sleep at midnight, we'll both go to sleep at ten") without both of you feeling the worse for it. The only solution is for each of you to cut the other a lot of slack where sleep is concerned. Going to bed separately, if you need to, won't hurt your marriage any. And, better rested, you'll feel more like having sex the next morning.

Eating is a different story altogether. Cultural and personal habits come into play much more strongly in influencing what and how we eat. For some people, meals are important interpersonal events: Meals are for talking and having a sense of togetherness. For other people, meals are simply events for eating, which can be done just as well on a tray in front of the TV as at the dining room table. A difference on that can be a problem, especially for the one who likes to eat more formally and make interpersonal contact with his or her partner at mealtime.

What to eat is often a bigger problem than how to eat. If you both love steak, that's OK. If you both prefer sprouts, that's OK too. But if one of you prefers steak and the other one prefers sprouts, that's not OK. There's a lot of potential for mutual disapproval there, especially if the difference turns into a prolonged argument about whose way is the "better" or "more sensible" way to live. Likewise, differences on other things that are usually categorized as "health habits"—smoking and exercise, for example—also make it hard for partners to affirm each other.

When partners differ on these things, they tend to pester each other about them: "How can you be so unconcerned about your health?" "How can *you* be so uptight? We only go around once, you know." And on and on. As with other differences between partners, differences on health-related items can trigger a cycle of polarization, with the partners becoming more and more extreme in their positions. What's worse, the person whose habits are more in what is commonly regarded as the healthful direction—lots of sprouts and exercise, no smoking—will feel morally justified in trying to change the other partner. Even though disaster lies at the end of that road, the temptation to follow it will be hard to resist. And if one of the partners meets up with someone of the opposite sex—at the gym, at the deli counter—whose health habits are more similar to their own, that partner will suddenly feel a wonderful sense of companionship that they hadn't been feeling, in this domain at least, with their partner. In short, having the same health habits is a great way to generate mutual affirmation, but having very different health habits is an easy way to generate conflict.

Now think about how you and your partner habitually go about maintaining your physical bodily selves. Focus in on that as a whole, and get a felt sense.

—How similar are you and your partner in how you go about maintaining your physical bodily selves?

Now it's time to put it all together for the major task of Maintaining Your Household. Think about it as a whole, focus in, and get a felt sense.

—How similar are you and your partner in your approach to Maintaining Your Household?

Filling Your Free Time

WHAT YOU DO. How you like to fill your free time depends on a combination of factors: your sex, your personality, and how you learned to fill your free time as you were growing up in your family. If, for example, when you were a kid, your father taught you how to fish, you may love it. If you weren't taught how to fish, you might wonder how anyone could spend all day in one place like that, "doing nothing."

When two people are dating, they can have fun and feel close doing almost anything. And what they do consists mostly of recreational activities—things that people can enjoy without being deeply interested in them: going to the movies, to dinner, dancing, and the like. They feel close not because of what they're doing but simply because they're together. What they're doing is just their excuse for being together. Everything is fun. That's the beauty of romantic love.

But once romantic love runs out of fuel, those "fun" things aren't automatically fun anymore. More important, they don't automatically produce the sense of closeness they did at the beginning. Think about the last time you were at a restaurant. Some of the couples were looking intently into each other's eyes, engaged in what seemed like deep, intimate conversation. But other couples were looking everywhere but at each other's eyes. And they hardly said a word to each other.

To keep on having fun together over the long haul, and to maintain a sense of closeness in your leisure time, it helps greatly to have at least one *serious shared interest:* something you both especially enjoy—something that for the two of you is "your thing," your *special* thing. (If you've got more than one serious shared interest, all the better.) It doesn't have to be something unusual—bird-watching or butterfly collecting or anything like that. It can even be one of those common recreational activities that people do when they're first dating, dancing, for instance. *What's important is that it's something you're both* so *interested in that it keeps you interested in each other.*

Sometimes partners are lucky enough to meet because of their serious shared interest: Marilee and Paul were both passionate Boston Red Sox fans. In fact they met at Fenway Park. It was a cold and rainy April night.

Each of them was sitting alone because the people they'd planned to go with had opted out due to the bad weather. Paul spotted Marilee working on her scorecard and said to himself, "Now, that's a fan!"⁵ He had met the woman of his dreams.

Of course, it often happens that partners who come into the marriage with a shared common interest develop new and different ones over the course of their life together. Ronald and Karen both enjoy working on houses. For some years, they've had the joint project of buying an old house, living in it, fixing it up, selling it, and then buying another old house and starting all over again. Neither came into the marriage knowing they liked to fix up houses; they had other serious shared interests. They discovered that they shared this one only after they bought their first house, a handyman special, which was all they could afford.

Having a serious shared interest is especially important if one of you has a serious interest that (a) your partner doesn't share and (b) takes up a lot of your time. If you two don't share a serious interest to counterbalance that nonshared interest, it will be easy for your partner to think that you love it, _____ (football, antiques, marathoning, gardening, working on your investments, bingo—fill in the blank), more than you love them. And it would be hard to blame your partner for having that thought. If you two do have a serious interest that you share, and spend a lot of time on it *together*, your partner will be reassured that even if you love _____, you don't love it more than you love them.

—How similar are you and your partner in what you most like to do in your free time? In particular, do you two have serious shared interests?

HOW YOU DO IT. Partners can be more or less alike not only in what they prefer to do in their free time but also in how they prefer to do it. I'm talking about four things here: (a) spending free time alone by themselves versus with each other; (b) spending time alone as a couple versus together with other couples; (c) doing exciting things versus quiet things; (d) doing expensive things versus inexpensive things.

The idea that men want more alone time and women want more together time is something that people take for granted as being true. It may well be. What partly accounts for our believing that it's true is the fact that many men are more interested in sports—especially watching sports on TV—than their partners are. And as I suggested before, if the woman doesn't have a serious interest of her own that can occupy the alone time created by her partner's long hours in front of the TV or at the driving range, there will be problems.

But even if sports or some other nonshared interest is not the issue, partners can still differ in their preferences for time alone versus time together. It's a matter of personality—and some women want more alone time than some men do. The tricky thing is that these differences might not be apparent during the early part of the relationship because when people are in romantic love they like to be together a lot, even people who are alone types deep down. So at this point you might not have a clear idea of how different you and your partner are on this. If you do feel unclear about it, then you and your partner have to talk about it. Once you've had that talk, focus in and get a felt sense.

—How similar are you and your partner in your preferences for time apart versus time together?

Some couples will tell you, "We don't socialize much," and some will tell you, "We socialize a lot." This is largely a matter of personality, too. I've known couples who were both introverted enough, and such good companions for each other, that they felt no need to socialize. They were perfectly content to spend all their free time alone together. On the other hand, there are couples who hardly ever spend their free time like that. They always want it to be a double date—or triple, or quadruple. They prefer that not because they can't have fun alone together—they can. It's just that they're both extroverts, and extroverts have the *most* fun when they're out among other people. (Then there are those couples who chose the wrong person and are bored in each other's company. They have to be out with other people to have any fun at all—but that's *not* going to be you.) Naturally, when someone who is very introverted marries someone who is the opposite, there is conflict about socializing, and it's hard to arrive at an arrangement that will be acceptable to both partners.

Introversion/extroversion also largely determines an individual's preference for spending his or her free time doing exciting things, such as going to nightclubs, versus doing quiet things at home, such as watching videos or playing Scrabble. So, as with socializing, when an introvert marries an extrovert, there is going to be conflict over doing exciting things versus quiet things, and it's going to have to be resolved somehow. But as with other differences on the Practical Dimension, small differences on introversion/extroversion can be enriching to both partners. The more extroverted partner can teach the more introverted one that sometimes it can be more fun to be out with other people. And the more introverted one can introduce the other to the pleasures of a quiet evening at home.

In some cases, partners are attracted to each other specifically because of a *big* difference between them on introversion/extroversion: The extroverted one seems so exciting and the introverted one seems so stable. But eventually that difference comes back to haunt them. The extroverted partner starts to think of the other partner as a stick-in-the-mud who stops them from really *living*. The introverted one starts to think of the other as superficial and childish. Their big difference on introversion/extroversion puts up a roadblock to the process of mutual affirmation.

There are tests you can take to tell you how introverted versus extroverted you are, but you don't need to take them. All the tests do is tell you what you told them first. You already know where you are on the introverted/extroverted continuum. And you know where your partner is, too. It doesn't take much experience with someone to know that. So reflect on that knowledge, and get a felt sense.

—How similar are you and your partner in your preference for socializing versus being alone together, and in your preference for doing exciting things versus quiet things?

Finally, people vary greatly in how much money they need to spend to have a good time. Some people prefer simple pleasures—inexpensive restaurants and balcony seats. Others need fancy restaurants and front-row seats to feel they're having a good time. And then there are all the people in the middle who like to splurge more or less often.

Obviously, how expensive your pleasures are will depend in large part on your income level. Rich people can, and do, indulge in more expensive pleasures than the rest of us. But it's not just a matter of money. Some rich people live very simply and some people with less money live very extravagantly. It's not exactly a matter of personality either. It's a matter of values, just as spending preferences are. A big difference between you and your partner on how much money it takes to have a good time is a very important difference. It signals that you and your partner's values are out of sync, and that in an important way you and your partner are not on the same wavelength.

—How similar are you and your partner in your attitudes about how much money it takes to have a good time?

That finishes the major task of Filling Your Free Time. Now it's time to consider that task as a whole, putting all its parts together. So, as with Spending Money, reflect on Filling Your Free Time as a whole, as if you had not first focused on its several aspects separately. Focus in and get a felt sense.

—How similar are you and your partner on the task of Filling Your Free Time?

Dealing with Your Families

Everyone who's lived to be three years old knows that family relationships are complicated. Your family relationships become doubly complicated as soon as you get married—correction: as soon as you get engaged, if not sooner. Now there are two families who are intensely curious about your private business; two families who generously offer you advice and expect you to follow it; two families who require your presence at times and places of their choosing—simultaneously, of course; two families who, sooner or later, will look to you for help in times of trouble.

How these complicated family relationships will play out for you and your partner will depend on a number of interacting factors: how much you like your family, how much they like you; how much you like your partner's family, how much they like you; how much your partner likes their own family, how much their family likes them; and so on. Then, when you consider that each of your families is composed of individuals, and that these individuals have their own unique, set of relationships with all the other family members, including you and your partner, you see how it gets even more complicated. But as I said, you already know that family relationships are complicated. You've lived it.

Family Cultures

Another thing you know from your own lived experience is how different from one another families can be. My friend Tim O'Connell, a psychologist and family therapist, once said, "Different families are like different countries. They speak different languages, they have different cultures." Different family cultures—different family traditions, different ways of going about everything that families do: maintaining contact, exchanging information, expressing affection, handling conflict, helping each other, and much more. For example, some families are "enmeshed." There's tremendous physical togetherness and everybody is in on everybody else's business. Other families are the opposite, "disengaged." Some families are loud and raucous when they fight, others are very subdued. In some families everyone is centered around a family project, a family business, for example, or their religious life. Other families don't have anything like that holding them together.

When partners actually do come from different countries or ethnic groups, it's no surprise if they find their partner's family culture different from their own. (You may remember that scene in *Annie Hall* in which Woody Allen's character is having a quiet dinner with Annie's well-mannered WASP family, and he compares that dinner, in his mind's eye, to the rowdy, chaotic mealtimes of his Jewish family in Brooklyn.) But it's not inevitable that partners from different ethnic groups will have very different family cultures. I've met plenty of couples who have found the culture of their partner's family surprisingly familiar and comfortable, despite differences in ethnicity. And partners from the same ethnic group can have totally different family cultures.

When partners do come from very different family cultures, it's harder for them to understand each other's behavior in relation to their family. This difficulty in mutual understanding can result in conflict. Tom and Annette are an example of such a couple.

Annette's father, Billy, was the classic American success story. He grew up in a tough neighborhood in New York: Hell's Kitchen. He dropped out of high school and took a job as a pin boy in a bowling alley. Eventually, after years of hard work and saving, and a lucky break, he opened his own bowling alley. Then in the early 1970s, he had the foresight to open a fitness club. His vision was of an upscale health club packed with amenities, and that is what he created. The Manhattan club was such a great success that he opened another, in the wealthy New Jersey suburb he'd moved to with his wife and four daughters.

The family that Billy and his wife created was very close-knit, with a strong family culture of working together, and of keeping everything that was important to the family under the family's control. By the time I met Billy's daughter, Annette, and her husband, Tom, Billy was semi-retired, dabbling in real estate, and Annette and her three sisters were running the health clubs. Since evenings and weekends were the busiest times for the health clubs, Annette was gone many evenings, leaving Tom, a federal employee with a nine-to-five job, to take care of their two kids when he got home. And at least once a week there was some kind of emergency that required Annette to be at the club on an evening she'd planned to be at home.

The family that Tom had grown up in had a very different family culture. It was much less enmeshed, quite disengaged, in fact. Tom's family was one where the players were cordial to each other but didn't have a lot to do with each other. Tom had a brother who lived only an hour away, but, in Tom's words, his brother was "living his own life." Tom's parents had retired to Arizona. He spoke to them briefly on the phone every week, but saw them only a couple of times a year. They, too, were living their own life. Because of the kind of family Tom came from, he was utterly unprepared for the huge time commitment, and emotional commitment, that Annette put into the health club and her family. He felt left out and resentful, and he and Annette had bitter fights about it. One day in my office Tom said, "You know, I've always felt like Number Three. Annette's family and the health club come first, the kids come second, and I come third."

Tom couldn't understand how Annette *had* to spend all that time in the health club. His family culture was too different from hers. If his family culture *had* been more similar, he might not have liked Annette's involvement with her family any better—chances are he wouldn't have—but he would have *understood* it. He would have been able to talk with Annette about his unhappiness more reasonably and productively, because he would have known, from his own family experience, what it felt like to be in her shoes.

I think it's an advantage if you and your partner come from similar family cultures. It will reduce the amount of conflict your families cause you because you'll generally agree on how your families should be dealt with. Even when you're caught in a tug-of-war between your two families—they both *must* have you for Thanksgiving dinner—you'll have less conflict because each of you will know how your partner feels being tugged like that.

If you've spent any time at all with your partner's family, on their turf, you already have an idea of how similar your partner's family culture is to yours. You know how familiar and comfortable it has felt for you to be with your partner's family, or how alien and awkward. Focus in on all that and get a felt sense.

—How similar is the family culture of your family to the family culture of your partner's family?

Think about being tugged by your family. Think about Annette being tugged by her family. What was her family hooking into that they could tug her like that? What is your family hooking into when they tug you? They are hooking into your *loyalty*.

Loyalty

Loyalty is what families are all about. Loyalty is the common currency in families. It's what the players count up at the end of the day. You measure every move you make in relation to your family against the yardstick of loyalty—whether you are conscious of it or not. And your family evaluates your every move in relation to them against the yardstick of loyalty—whether they are conscious of it or not.

What is loyalty, anyway? A simple definition, in a family context, is this: You are loyal to your family when you act according to your family's standards, expectations, and wishes, *even, and especially, when those standards, expectations, and wishes run counter to your own.*

I consider loyalty to be an admirable quality in general, including loyalty to your family, *if that's possible for you.* It may not be possible, though, for you to be loyal to your family because they have been disloyal to you—by lying to you, for example, or by mentally, physically, or sexually abusing you. If you can't be loyal to your family, that's OK. But if you are loyal to your family at all, and especially if you are very loyal to your family, you must bear one thing in mind. This thing is so very important that I'm going to state it as a rule:

The Loyalty Rule
No matter how loyal you have always been to your family, once you get married you must transfer your *primary* loyalty to the new family that you and your partner have created by the act of getting married.

Indeed, one of the several neat tricks you have to pull off to be happily married is to transfer your *primary* loyalty to your partner while remaining loyal *enough* to your family.[6] Lots of different kinds of happy marriages are possible, but one thing all happy marriages have in common is that the partners have transferred their primary loyalty to their marriage.

In order to do this, one of the first things you and your partner have to do after you get married is to build a protective wall around the *new* family that you two have just created. That wall is built of two things: *information* and *commitments*.

INFORMATION. You and your partner have to agree on what information you will pass on to your families, and what information you won't because it's too sensitive. You have to agree on what kinds of information you will *never* share with your families. (Details of your sexual relationship are a likely example.) And you have to decide on exactly when and how to share the information that you don't withhold from your families. For example, if you have to make an important decision—whether to take a new job that's been offered you, or to buy a particular house, or to move to a different state—do you discuss that decision with family members beforehand? Do you ask them for advice? Or do you and your partner make your decision first, and tell your families about it only afterward? And if you do discuss the decision with family members beforehand, how do you do it—together as a couple, or separately with your respective families?

If you and your partner come from different family cultures, you have likely developed very different habits about information exchange with your families. These different habits can cause nasty conflicts if you two haven't agreed on how to maintain your protective loyalty wall when it comes to information. There are some people, for example, who regard one of their parents as their closest confidant. (Remember Anthony Perkins in *Psycho* saying to Janet Leigh, "A boy's best friend is his mother"? Not as extreme as that, obviously, but something along those lines.) If you don't have a close, confiding relationship with either of your parents, you will certainly feel that your partner's long daily phone calls with Mother are a violation of the boundaries of your relationship. You might not mind these calls so much if *your* best friend is your mother.

Jacob and Liza had been married for several years, and were having trouble conceiving. It appeared that the problem had to do with Liza's reproductive system. Although rationally Liza knew that the fertility problem was not her fault, she felt like a failure and felt terribly guilty and ashamed over it. Tests finally established that the problem concerned Liza's fallopian tubes, and the decision was made to try in vitro fertilization (IVF).

Jacob's parents were eager to have a grandchild, and Jacob and Liza had indicated to them, two years before, that they were trying to conceive. Ever since then, at least once a month, Jacob's parents would take him aside and ask, "How are you and Liza doing?" which was code for "Is Liza pregnant yet—if not, why not?" All his life, Jacob had been used to confiding in his parents, but knowing Liza's wishes, all he would say in reply was "We're working on it." Finally, and for just a moment, after the third attempt at IVF had failed, Jacob lost his discipline and told his parents about the fertility problem. For that moment Jacob felt great relief, as he'd always felt when telling his parents about a problem, but simultaneously he knew he was making a huge mistake. Liza was, indeed, mortified by Jacob's having told his parents something that even her own parents didn't know. Ironically, just a month later Liza and Jacob learned that their fourth attempt at IVF had succeeded. If only Jacob had maintained his and Liza's loyalty wall just a little longer, Liza wouldn't have had to suffer needless humiliation.

Notice that I can't tell you how much information you have to withhold to maintain your protective loyalty wall. No one can; it's totally subjective. It's for you and your partner to decide whether you need the Great Wall of China, only a couple of courses of brick, or something in between.

—How closely do you and your partner agree on what to do about information to maintain the protective loyalty wall around your marriage?

COMMITMENTS. Your protective loyalty wall is also composed of the commitments that you make (or don't make) to your families. By commitments I mean the things that you do for your families. I don't just mean things that you do *with* your families, like inviting them to dinner or attending family functions. I also mean the things that you do in living your own personal life because your family wants you to do them— things that you do for their sake but wouldn't do otherwise. An example of that kind of commitment would be raising your children in the religious tradition that is meaningful to your parents, even though that tradition doesn't mean very much to you.

The commitments you make to your families vary in scale from small ones like attending family dinners, to large ones like taking a leave from work to help a family member who's recovering from an illness or operation, to even larger ones like financing a family member's college education or taking in a widowed parent to live with you permanently.

You and your partner have to agree on which commitments you're willing to make to your families, which commitments you're not willing to make, and on how you as a couple go about making these commitments, because differences between you on these issues can cause serious conflict. Dan's parents expected him to visit every Sunday and he felt he couldn't say no, even though spending every Sunday with them was not his idea of a good time. He very much wanted his wife, Jeannie, to come with him just so he'd have a little more fun on those visits. Jeannie couldn't understand how Dan could feel so obligated to his parents; she'd never felt that kind of obligation with her parents. When, for Dan's sake, she accompanied him to his parents' house on Sundays, she resented losing her Sunday. When she stayed home, she resented losing Dan for half their weekend. One day in exasperation she said to him, "You're more their son than you are my husband. I hate it." This was a difference on what I'd consider a small-scale commitment but it generated a lot of conflict. Differences on larger-scale commitments are all the more destructive.

If you and your partner have been together awhile, you've probably had to deal with some small-scale commitments. You may have already had to deal with large commitments. You may even have had to deal with very large commitments—for example, if your families object to you marrying out of your faith. It may be, though, that large-scale commitments to your families are only hypothetical at this point. But what if your sister did ask you and your partner for a large loan? Or what if your partner's widowed father couldn't cope on his own and his choices were either to live with you or in a nursing home? Decisions on large-scale commitments like these are likely to come up sooner or later, so it's important for you and your partner to talk about them as soon as possible.

As with releasing information to your families, it's not how much in the way of commitments you're willing to make that counts. What counts is that you and your partner agree on what you're willing to take on, whether that is a lot or a little. Now it's time for you to reflect on loyalty, as it is expressed in commitments. Focus in and get a felt sense.

—How closely do you and your partner agree on handling commitments to your families so that you maintain the loyalty boundary around your new family?
—In particular, how closely do you and your partner agree on the largest-scale commitments you are prepared to make for your own and the other's families?

And now it's time for you to focus in on the major task of dealing with your families as a whole. Put it all together and get a felt sense.

—How close are you and your partner on the major task of Dealing with Your Families?

THOSE ARE ALL the defining questions for the Practical Dimension. It's time for you to focus in on your experience working through this chapter, and to get a felt sense of you and your partner on the Practical Dimension *overall*. Do not focus in on specific aspects of the dimension or specific hand rotations. And please do not try to come up with some arithmetical average of your hand rotations. Instead, imagine yourself in an airplane, flying over your experience of this chapter and being able to see all of it, all at once. Focus in and get a felt sense of all that.

—How close are you and your partner on the Practical Dimension?

Please *do* make a note of how far you moved your hands in this hand rotation.

Dialogue

Now it's time for you and your partner to get together and talk about your felt sense of compatibility on the Practical Dimension:

1) Find a quiet place where you can sit across from each other at a table.
2) Simultaneously show each other your hand rotation for that last defining question, on the Practical Dimension as a whole.
3) Each of you translate your hand rotation into words, using just a sentence or two—for example, "I feel wonderfully close to you on this dimension and I think we'll really be able to affirm each other on it," or "I'm just a little nervous about it. We'll have some problems about it, but I think we'll be OK," or "I'm really worried about it. I think it will be hard for us to affirm each other on this dimension."
4) Take turns in bringing up an aspect of the dimension that's of particular concern to you. Describe the experiences you two have had on it that cause you concern. Describe how you think your differences on it might affect your marriage. Describe what would have to be different about you, your partner, and your relationship so that you would not be as concerned with that aspect of the dimension. Take as many turns as you need to bring up all your concerns.
5) Go through the chapter together and mention anything—positive as

well as negative—that occurred to you when you went through the chapter individually.

6) When you and your partner have finished your dialogue and you're by yourself again, focus in on that last defining question, on the Practical Dimension as a whole, get a felt sense, and express it to yourself with your hands. If you have read *Focusing* and learned to do all six focusing movements, then do a full focusing session on the felt sense that you just experienced.

10

THE SEXUAL DIMENSION

A cartoon in *The New Yorker* went something like this: Bride and groom standing at the altar looking somewhat taken aback. Minister saying to them, "Do you, Jason, swear that you will not have sexual relations with anybody except Judy for as long as you both shall live? And do you, Judy, swear that you will not have sexual relations with anybody except Jason for as long as you both shall live?"

That's what we're talking about when we talk about monogamy. It's a tall order. We all know that sexual interest is, for many of us, promiscuous. We know that novelty lends an extra kick to sexuality. Every day we encounter people who are physically attractive and sexually intriguing. At the very least, we can't help but be curious about what sex would be like with them.

We are not alone. Among mammals in general, novelty—that is, replacing an old partner with a new one—is the surefire way to maintain high rates of sexual behavior. There are good evolutionary reasons for this, having to do with maintaining diversity in the gene pool.

If we're honest with ourselves, we know that the promiscuity of our sexual interest won't disappear simply because we've gotten married. But if we take our marriage vows seriously, we are committing ourselves to *not being promiscuous at all* in our behavior *for the rest of our lives*—just like the man said in the cartoon. It seems as though marriage requires of us something that goes against our essential nature. That might well be the case.

An option that some of us choose is to marry but not be monogamous. That is not an option I can recommend. It's not my job, as a psychologist, to give you a moral argument about why infidelity is bad. You have enough other people moralizing at you about that. I'll just share a clinical observation: In my work with torture survivors and with people who have lost a child, I have seen the face of anguish. The only other people in whom I've seen anything even approaching that anguish are people who have been cheated on by their husband or their wife.

Given that nonmonogamy is not an option, the trick for married people is to maintain an interesting and satisfying sex life without resorting to novel partners. It's a neat trick, but one that happily married couples manage year in and year out. They can do it because they match up closely on the Sexual Dimension. That is, they match up well in three related but different ways:

—Comfort with Sexuality
—Interest in Sex
—Sexual Style

Let's take a close look at each of these three components of the Sexual Dimension.

Comfort with Sexuality

By "comfort with sexuality," I mean simply how relaxed you are about doing all the various things people do that are connected with sex: thinking about it, reading about it, watching movies about it, talking about it, telling jokes about it, as well as actually doing it. Like any other complex personality trait, comfort with sexuality results from the intricate interplay of a number of factors: the attitudes about sex that you learned in your family as you grew up, early cultural influences such as childhood religious training, later cultural influences including influences from peers and from the media, and your actual sexual experiences (both before and after puberty)—all of these interacting with the temperamental and personality factors that make up the rest of who you are.

People generally learn to become more comfortable with sexuality as they mature. Doing just that is one of the important developmental tasks of growing up. Yet, it's clear that by the time we reach adulthood, some of us are more comfortable with sexuality than others.

When someone is not very comfortable with sexuality it's not necessarily due to lack of experience. Clarence, for example, told me that when he was in college there was open competition among his fraternity brothers over who could "nail" the most coeds. He'd "nailed" quite a few himself, in slam-bam-thank-you-ma'am encounters that were over very quickly, that didn't mean anything to him, and that he didn't even enjoy very much. Despite all his "sexual experience," Clarence had considerable anxiety, uncertainty, and confusion connected with sex, and he hadn't been able to fashion a satisfying sexual relationship with his wife.

Conversely, people don't necessarily have to have a great deal of sexual experience to be comfortable with sexuality. Many are comfortable with it from the start. When people are not comfortable with sexuality it's less likely to be due to inexperience than to other factors such as having been taught in childhood that sex is dirty or bad, disliking or being ashamed of their own body, or being squeamish about all sorts of things having to do with the body in general.[1] People can also be uncomfortable with sexuality as a result of the tragic experience of having been sexually abused in childhood.

An individual can be comfortable with some aspects of sexuality but not others. Often these discrepancies are inconsequential, as when someone who is generally comfortable with sexuality is embarrassed watching love scenes in movies. Sometimes, these discrepancies do have consequences. Wilbur is an example: Wilbur's problem was that he wasn't turned on by his wife in the way he was to women he saw in hotel lobbies and airport terminals. He would have fantasies about "having his way" with these women. He felt he couldn't have sex that way with his wife. Wilbur was careful to point out that the trouble was not with his wife— she was beautiful, sexually attractive to him, and she certainly enjoyed sex. When I asked Wilbur what "having his way" consisted of, he didn't describe anything particularly kinky. He simply meant being a little less inhibited about sex than he characteristically was with his wife. For instance, in his fantasies Wilbur imagined talking dirty during sex. I suggested to Wilbur that he ask his wife if she might like it if he did that with her. He replied that he couldn't possibly talk with his wife about doing that. I asked him why not, and he replied that he just couldn't—it made him too embarrassed and nervous. He'd never talked to any of his partners about sex—just did it with them. By having Wilbur repeatedly visualize talking to his wife about talking dirty, and taking him through some worst-case analysis about it, I was able to persuade him to do it. To Wilbur's delight, his wife told him that she thought she'd like it if he talked dirty to her during sex. Progressively, Wilbur was able to tell her about the other things he fantasized doing, and to his delight and amazement, his wife responded positively every time. Once the ice was broken, Wilbur and his wife were able to engage in an ongoing dialogue about their sexual relationship, which enhanced it for both of them.

Ideally, you and your partner would match up on comfort with sexuality because you are both very comfortable with it. Small differences between the two of you in comfort with sexuality are OK too, as long as the less comfortable one is nevertheless reasonably comfortable with it. Differences between partners within the reasonably comfortable range can be worked on and worked out. But if one of you is quite uncomfortable with sexuality, it's better if *both* of you are quite uncomfortable with sexuality than if one of you is much more comfortable with it than the other. If there is a big difference between partners in how comfortable they are with sexuality, they will both feel sexually lonely, and ultimately they will feel resentful. The more comfortable one will feel frustrated, disappointed, and deprived. The less comfortable one will feel pressured, guilty, and inadequate. The partners' negative feelings about their sex life will seep into the rest of their relationship. Some of the most unhappy couples I have ever met, couples who had progressed beyond anger to hate, had a difference in comfort with sexuality at the root of their problems. Generally, they barely acknowledged it, if at all—it was too terribly painful—but it was there, and it had poisoned their relationship.

It is actually better for partners to be matched at a low level of comfort with sexuality because then they will both feel sexually *safe*. They may not have a great sex life, by other people's standards, but neither will they get caught in the vicious spiral of frustration, disappointment, guilt, inadequacy, and resentment that is the fate of couples who are poorly matched on comfort with sexuality.

You know your own level of comfort with sexuality. And by now you've had enough sexual experience with your partner to have an idea of how sexually comfortable they are.

—How closely do you and your partner match up on comfort with sexuality?

Interest in Sex

By "interest in sex," I mean simply how preoccupied you are with it and how often you want to do it—not just with respect to your current partner, right now, but as a general thing. Clearly, your interest in sex will be influenced by how comfortable you are with sexuality. If you're quite comfortable sexually, then it's likely that you'll be thinking about sex more, and wanting to do it more, than someone who is not very comfortable with sexuality.

But sex is not just psychological. It is physical, biological. And so it's safe to presume that interest in sex, in the sense of *sex drive*, as it's commonly called, is partly influenced by heredity just as other physical traits such as height and eye color are. (We should bear in mind, though, that as an inherited trait, sex drive, which can be influenced by our early experiences and environment—via our comfort with sexuality—is more like height, which can be strongly influenced by environmental conditions, such as diet, than it is to eye color.)

It is well known that inherited traits vary greatly from individual to individual. It is also known that traits that are measurable in terms of amount, like height and weight, vary in a predictable way, according to what statisticians call a "normal curve" (Figure 4). The horizontal axis shows the range of scores for a trait and the vertical axis shows the number of individuals at a given score. (If this were a normal curve for sex drive, then people with very high sex drive would be at the far right, and people with very low sex drive would be at the far left.) As you can see, for a normally distributed trait, most people are clustered in the average range. There are progressively fewer people with scores that are farther away, in either direction, from the mean score (also called the average). What is true for other human traits is likely true for sex drive: Most people fall in the middle somewhere, with fewer off to the extremes.

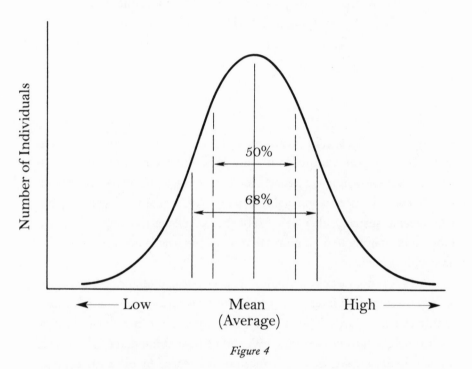

Figure 4

So the good news is that, as a matter of statistical probability, it's likely that you and your partner are reasonably well matched on sex drive. You're both somewhere in the middle. Every once in a while, though, couples are poorly matched: One partner is at one of the extremes—or worse, one is at each extreme. That mismatch may not be evident at the very beginning of the relationship, because in the romantic phase, when the sex is new, it is frequent. The mismatch becomes evident only later, when sexual novelty has faded a bit.

I've met couples with a variety of mismatches. Karla, for example, had a fairly high sex drive, but her husband, Lawrence, had a low sex drive. It wasn't that he had hang-ups about sex— he didn't. Whenever he and Karla had sex, he really enjoyed it. And afterward he would wonder to himself, "This is so much fun. Why don't I feel like doing it more often?" Karla loved Lawrence dearly and couldn't imagine living without him. At the same time, going outside the marriage for sex was morally unacceptable to her. She was in a real bind. Here's another example: Irena had a high sex drive, and Rodney had a very, very high sex drive. This difference wasn't a problem for them at the start. Their wonderful sexual connection was one of the things that they valued most, and in the beginning it seemed perfectly natural to be having sex multiple times a day. After a while, though, Irena started to feel exhausted and worn-out by their sexual frequency. She still wanted to have sex frequently by most people's standards, but not frequently enough for Rodney, who wanted to maintain the same frantic pace they'd had at the start. Irena felt guilty about not wanting sex enough, and Rodney felt guilty about wanting sex too much.

Differences in sex drive are like the differences in sleep needs that I mentioned in the last chapter: It's crucial for you to understand that this is simply how your partner is; that they can't just will themselves into having a higher or lower sex drive. But the remedy that works for differences in sleep needs—letting each partner do his or her own thing—doesn't work for differences in sex drive, because sex is something that people (ideally) do with their partner rather than by themselves. If you and your partner differ greatly in your sex drive, you're going to have to talk with each other about that and see if you can come up with some clever ways to bridge that difference. But then again, the chances are good that you two are similar enough in your sex drive.

I want to emphasize that what I am talking about is your abiding, baseline level of sexual desire, not how much you feel like having sex on any particular day. That varies a lot, and it's influenced by many factors aside from your biological level of sexual need. Most important, it's influenced by how well you and your partner are getting along in general— whether you're feeling mellow and close or angry and distant. It's also influenced by your energy level, the amount of time you and your partner are able to spend alone together cultivating your relationship, and how much stress you're under from your job and other responsibilities. Sex requires physical effort and mental concentration. When we're exhausted and stressed-out, we may have only enough energy to watch TV or flip through a magazine.

Finally, I want to emphasize that I'm not saying it's necessary to have high sexual interest and frequency to have a satisfying sex life. Couples who are matched at a low level of sex drive have perfectly fine sexual relationships. They don't have sex as frequently as other people, but when they do have sex it's exciting and enjoyable, and it reaffirms their bond with each other.

At this point in your relationship, it may be hard for you to have a clear sense of how well you and your partner match up on sexual interest. It may be that your opportunities to have sexual contact are infrequent enough so that whenever you get together you both really feel like doing it. Or it may be that it's early enough in your relationship so that your sexual frequency is naturally very high because of the superabundant sexual energy of romantic love. But if you think you can focus in and get a felt sense about your and your partner's level of sexual interest, now is the time to do it.

—How similar are you and your partner in your level of sexual interest?

Sexual Style

Each of us has our own personal style. We express that personal, individual, style in almost everything we do: how we walk, how we talk, how we sign our name, how we hold the steering wheel when we drive, how we dress and wear our hair, how we do our makeup or make a jump shot—just about everything.

Our personal style is especially important when it comes to expressing emotions. Creative artists—painters, writers, musicians—can't express their own, personal emotions until they discover their own personal style for doing it. That style is embodied in the tiniest gestures, such as the shape of a brush stroke. (Duke Ellington's touch on the piano was so distinctive that you could tell it was him and no one else by hearing him strike just one note.)

We know that when we want to express our love to our partner, we have our own personal style for doing that. We each have our own unique combination of gestures, actions, words, and phrases, which convey not just our love but also who, exactly, we are in conveying that love.

Likewise, each of us has our own personal, individual, sexual style. That style conveys who we uniquely are during sex. Our personal sexual style derives from two deep sources. First, it derives from our sense of what sex is—what it's primarily for, what it's primarily about. For some of us, sex is primarily about expressing love and experiencing the most profound emotional connection that we can have with another person. For some of us, sex is primarily about experiencing sexual pleasure and discovering new and better ways of achieving that. Some of us conceptualize sex as primarily a means for conceiving new life; some of us conceptualize it as a relaxation technique, a way to cope with stress. For some of us, sex is a solemn, serious, almost mystical thing, and for some of us sex is a form of play and can even be comical at times. For some of us, sex is an elevated experience. For some of us, sex is down and dirty, and we like it that way. And for some of us, what sex is primarily about—connection or pleasure, conception or relaxation—and how sex is—serious or comic, elevated or dirty—changes from one sexual encounter to another, even if all of our sexual encounters are with the same partner.

The second, related source of our personal sexual style is in the kind of identity, or identities, we want to take on during sex. Some of us want to take on a strong, masterful, dominating identity during sex—even if we are not characteristically like that in the other domains of our life. Some of us want to take on a passive, submissive role—again, even if we're not like that in the rest of our life. Some of us go into a trancelike state, as if part of us were off somewhere else. Others of us take an active, engaged role during sex; we're *right there* every second, speaking to our partner and looking into their eyes. Some of us take on an immature, childlike role during sex; others of us couldn't imagine being that way during sex. Some of us want to, and are able to, take on different sexual identities from one sexual encounter to the other.

Whatever your sexual style, it is crucially important that your partner's sexual style meshes with yours. That doesn't mean that your sexual partner's style must be identical to yours. All it means is that your partner's style, whatever it is, has to fit well enough with yours so that you can enact and express your style freely. If your style and your partner's style don't mesh well enough, each of you will feel that your partner is cramping your style. Each of you will feel that sex isn't *what* you want it to be, and that you can't be *who* you want to be sexually. Specifically, you will find yourself not being able to do the sexual things you really want to do, or worse, doing sexual things that you really don't want to do.

Fabian and Pamela were a couple whose sexual styles didn't mesh. For Pamela, sex was primarily about relieving sexual tension. She liked sex fast, and she liked it rough. And she preferred to take a somewhat disengaged role, emotionally, during sex. For Fabian, on the contrary, sex was primarily about connection. He liked it slow, and he liked it tender. Pamela had no patience for that, and Fabian missed the sense of connection he craved when they had sex Pamela's way. (It may sound like I switched the genders in this example, but I didn't. So, who's from what planet?)

Your sexual style, like so much about your sexuality, is determined in part by your level of comfort with sexuality. People can evolve a new and different sexual style, in a relationship where they trust their partner sexually, as they become more sexually comfortable. For example, people for whom sex was initially about connection and whose identity was trancelike can develop a sexual style in which sex is more frankly about pleasure, and in which they can take on a role that is less trancelike and more engaged. But that kind of evolution can happen only in a relationship where there is sexual trust, and that trust develops much more easily when the partners' sexual styles mesh well in the first place.

It may be that you have never thought about sex explicitly in terms of style before. You may have used different words for it, but you know what I mean. Inevitably, you've had the occasion to reflect on how satisfying a sexual encounter was, even if it consisted only of a kiss. It may even be that you've been on the receiving end of the question "Was it good for you, too?" and felt a slight pang as you answered, "Oh, yes."

—To what degree does your sexual style mesh with your partner's sexual style?

Now that we've gone through the three components of the Sexual Dimension, you could focus in right now and get a felt sense of how close you and your partner are on it. But I'd rather you didn't do that just yet. Before that, I think it's important for you to take a close and unflinching look at two aspects of yourself as a sexual being.

Your Sexual Requirements

<u>LOOKS.</u> One of the great things about our lives as human beings is that our partner doesn't have to look like a supermodel (whether male or female) for us to regard them as beautiful. The fact that beauty *is* in the eye of the beholder works in our favor. We regard members of the opposite sex who look very different from each other as beautiful, and we're attracted to all of them. We understand that there are many different ways for people to look beautiful and to appeal to us. Of course, we are ready, willing, and able to rank members of the opposite sex along some abstract scale of good looks. But when it comes to our *personal* preferences, all that matters is that someone be in our *ballpark* for good looks. That ballpark includes all the different kinds of people whose looks appeal to us. It doesn't matter if someone is in a box seat or in the bleachers. If they're in the ballpark, their looks appeal to us, and we're sexually attracted to them.

It's probably obvious to you that the person whom you marry must be someone you consider to be physically and sexually attractive. It's not obvious to everybody. The problem with these people is not necessarily that they don't consider physical and sexual attractiveness to be important. They do. They *feel* that importance. The problem these people have is that they *think* that physical and sexual attractiveness in a partner *should not be* important to them. They may say to themselves that it is uncivilized and unworthy—animalistic somehow—to place so much emphasis on the physical when there is so much more to a person than that. They may feel guilty that they are not that attracted to their partner physically and sexually, when their partner is so wonderful in so many other ways. They feel ashamed by the strength of their sexual urges, and think they should not be so strongly controlled by their animal instincts.

But we *are* animals. And if we are sexually alive at all, then, inevitably, looks *do* matter. If we somehow end up marrying someone who really isn't, in our eyes, good-looking and sexually attractive, our lives inevitably come to feel bleak and not fully alive. Consequently, it's very important for you to be honest with yourself about whether your partner is someone who truly is physically and sexually attractive to you—that your partner is in your ballpark. And, whether your ballpark for attractiveness is large or small, you must feel legitimate and moral about *wanting* a partner who is in that ballpark. It's a matter of feeling fully alive.

There's an opera in which the devil convinces a naive young man that he should free himself of his animal instincts, and so persuades him to marry a bearded lady. Soon enough, the young man realizes he's made a Big Mistake.[2] As long as you acknowledge the legitimacy and importance of your sexual requirements, you'll never make that kind of mistake.

Now, if I were to ask you, "Is your partner in your ballpark for looks?" chances are you would instantly reply, "Absolutely!" If that wouldn't be your instant reply, then it would be a good idea for you to ask yourself that question again *and feel your way to your answer.*

SEXUAL PASSION. Just as it's important for you to feel that it is legitimate and moral to want a partner who is physically attractive to you, it's important to feel the same way about wanting a partner with whom you can have sexual experiences that are as fulfilling and exciting *as you know* you *are capable of having.* To do that, you have to be clear about the difference between sexual experiences that are warm, close, and romantic, and those that are high in sexual power and passion. Ideally, sexual experiences are both romantic and sexually powerful. But if sex with your current partner is romantic but not as sexually powerful as it has been for you with a previous partner, you have to be honest with yourself about whether that will be good enough for you over the long run. Sometimes people convince themselves that it will be good enough, only to find out later that they had been kidding themselves.[3]

That's what happened to Wendy. Her previous relationship, with Walter, had been volatile, chaotic, and ultimately very painful. But the sex was always great—powerful and passionate, whether she and Walter were loving each other or hating each other. Her present relationship, with Todd, was very different. In contrast to the emotional roller coaster with Walter, Wendy's relationship with Todd was calm, steady, and emotionally reassuring, and she deeply loved him for that. But sex with Todd was nothing like it had been with Walter. It was warm and tender—and it was enjoyable as such—but it was missing the passion that she had experienced with Walter. Initially, her reaction was "Passionate, powerful sex? Been there, done that. This is just fine." But after a while, Wendy began to realize how important sexual passion was to her. She realized that she couldn't live the rest of her life without it, and that what she had to do was find a partner who combined the emotional qualities of Todd with the sexual qualities of Walter.

In thinking about your own sexual requirements, you, like Wendy, have to think comparatively. In comparison with other sexual relationships you've had, how sexually powerful is your relationship with your present partner? How much of what you most need and want—and know you can have—in a sexual relationship do you experience with your present partner?

Once you've reflected on your answers to these questions, and reflected about your ballpark for physical attractiveness, you can focus on the next defining question. Notice that I don't ask you to do the Hand-Rotation Exercise in response to it. You may think about the answer to this question in terms of more versus less, but I think the answer is either yes or no.

—Does your partner meet your sexual requirements?

Your Readiness for Monogamy

Consider the following two questions:
—How bothered are you by the idea that you haven't had enough sexual experience, with enough people, now that you are thinking about getting married?

—How bothered are you by the idea of giving up the chance to have sex with anyone but your partner for the rest of your life, once you get married?

Notice that these two questions are not the same question. The first deals with the past, the second with the future. We all grapple with these questions as we think about getting married. The cartoon I mentioned at the start of this chapter is about these questions. That's why we think it's funny.

The first question boils down to "Do you think that you've sown enough wild oats?" Your answer depends partly on the amount of wild oats you've sown, but also on your evaluation of those experiences compared with what you've experienced with your current partner. The better you feel about your current sexual relationship, the easier it will be for you to say "been there, done that" about the sex you've had with others, and really mean it.

The second question is trickier—and it is the bottom-line question. Your answer depends much less on the amount and variety of sexual experience you've had up to now, and much more on *who you are as a sexual being*. Most of us are bothered, at least a little, by the idea of "forsaking all others" for the rest of our life. That's a long time and a lot of missed opportunities—but we can imagine doing it, we do it, and we succeed at it.

Some people cannot even imagine forsaking all others. They know they could never succeed at it, no matter how much sexual experience and how many partners they've already had. Prescott is that kind of person. He's handsome and successful. But more than that, he's a very nice man, a very warm and sweet man. Prescott would make a terrific husband and father—except he knows, and has known for a long time, that he could never be faithful to one partner. It's not that he hasn't had enough, or varied enough, sexual experiences. By his mid twenties, he was way into the double digits in sexual partners. Prescott is in his late forties now, *and he's still at it.*

Long ago, Prescott realized that he was his father's son. He knew how his father had repeatedly broken his mother's heart with his incessant infidelities. And he knew, deep down in his soul, that he wouldn't be any more successful at fidelity, if he were married, than his father had been. Early on, he decided that he would never break a woman's heart the way his father had broken his mother's. The solution was obvious: never get married. Prescott is not entirely happy with this solution. He wishes he could have gotten married and had children. But he's certain that, because of who he is sexually, marriage would be disastrous, both for him and for the woman he married.

Your readiness for monogamy is much greater than Prescott's. Otherwise, you wouldn't be reading this book. But it's worthwhile to reflect on just how ready for monogamy you are—how ready you really are to forsake *all others*.

—How ready are you for monogamy?

Now that you've considered your own sexual requirements and your readiness for monogamy, you're in a better position to get an accurate felt sense of you and your partner on the Sexual Dimension.

—How close are you and your partner on the Sexual Dimension?

Before you and your partner engage in dialogue about the Sexual Dimension, I want to emphasize something that I said earlier in the book.

As I mentioned in chapter 2, and as you already know anyway, a truth that many people hold to be self-evident is that sooner or later, once you get married, your sex life starts to go downhill, and it continues to go downhill—inevitably and unstoppably—forever. It doesn't have to be that way. It isn't that way for many, many couples. That's not to say that sex is great all the time for these couples, no matter what. Sexual relationships are too fragile for that. Even for couples with an excellent sexual relationship, over the long run there will be periods where the sex isn't so good. Those periods can last for weeks, months, even a couple of years before the partners get back on track. A great variety of things can cause a couple's sexual relationship to cool off for a while: job stress, financial worries, pregnancy, children, and all the other factors that can cause stress and conflict in relationships. So, if we were to graph the quality of a couple's long-term sexual relationship, the line wouldn't be straight. It would be wavy, reflecting the inevitable ups and downs in the couple's sexual relationship over many years. But the *trend* of the line (represented by the dotted lines in Figure 5) is not downward. It is steady. It can even slope upward, as the partners gain confidence and maturity, learn more and more about themselves and each other sexually, and create an ever-more powerful and deep sexual relationship together.

A friend of mine, Mike, once said to me that the great thing about music is that it is infinite. What he meant was that, even though the notes themselves are always the same, musicians are constantly putting them together in new ways that give us new and illuminating experiences. To put what Mike said a bit differently, musical *exploration* is infinite.

Figure 5

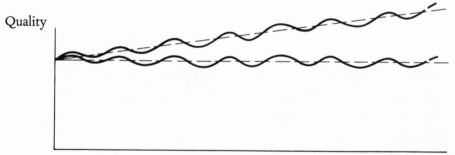

The same is true for sex. Sex is infinite; sexual exploration is infinite. Doing that exploration via new partners has its obvious appeal. Monogamy has this advantage: With a new partner, you are always back to "Go" again, no matter how exciting the sex with your new partner is. You are back at the preparatory stage for sexual exploration—just learning the basics about your partner's sexuality, just beginning to get comfortable with your own sexuality around this new partner. In a long-term monogamous relationship, you and your partner are long past the preparatory stage for sexual exploration. You're equipped for it with the knowledge of each other's sexuality that you've acquired over the years, and with the sexual trust to take the risk of venturing together deep into uncharted sexual territory. As Bette Midler said, it gets better as you get older—as long as you and your partner are close on the Sexual Dimension.

Dialogue

Sex is hard for all of us to talk about, to one degree or another. So before you and your partner engage in dialogue about the Sexual Dimension, you've got to make sure that you feel comfortable enough to do it. You know how to make sure that you're comfortable enough: by focusing. Get an image of you and your partner discussing the Sexual Dimension and see what felt sense comes up. Then get a handle on it. You might identify the feeling as anything from terror to just the very slightest apprehension. Once you've identified the feeling, then you can decide, based on it, whether you are comfortable enough to discuss the Sexual Dimension with your partner right now. If you decide you are comfortable enough, then skip the next two paragraphs (unless you're curious, in which case, be my guest).

If you are not comfortable enough, then you have to decide whether that's because talking about sex in general is uncomfortable for you, or if it's because there's something so troubling to you about your own sexuality, or your partner's, that you can't imagine talking about it. If it's just that you're uncomfortable talking about sex in general, you can cure that. All you have to do is read some good sexual material *aloud* with your partner. I've included a good book on sexuality in "For Further Reading" at the end of this book. You could read the books out loud together from beginning to end or pick chapters that seem particularly relevant to you. You'll find, as everyone does, that reading books on sexuality aloud together is a reassuring and liberating experience.

If the problem is that you are troubled by some aspect of your own or your partner's sexuality, first consider the possibility that talking about it, once you start, might be easier than you anticipate. Next, consider carefully the negative consequences of raising your concerns now—the anxiety and embarrassment—compared with the consequences for your sexual future if you don't raise those concerns now. My guess is that going through the pain now will spare you a great deal more pain later. It may be helpful for you, too, to read books on sexuality aloud with your partner. Not only will it make you more relaxed in talking about sex, but some of the specific points in the books may give you ideas for exactly how you could express your particular concerns.

Sex is a sensitive subject for all of us. To make sure that you and your partner can have an informative dialogue about the Sexual Dimension without anyone's feelings being hurt, it's important for each of you to take care to talk about *yourself* rather than about your partner. The instructions for this dialogue are designed to promote that kind of self-focused discussion:

1) Find a quiet place where you can sit across from each other at a table.
2) Flip a coin to determine who's going to talk first. Then take turns talking with each other about what you *value* about your sexual relationship with your partner. I would suggest this frame for doing that: "One thing I value about our sexual relationship is that *we . . .*" Each of you should mention one thing at a time in your turn, and then let the other mention one thing he or she values. Keep on alternating until you are done.
3) Simultaneously show each other your hand rotations for that last defining question, about the Sexual Dimension as a whole. Do *not* try to put that hand rotation into words.
4) Discuss your comfort with sexuality. (Whoever wants to go first on this one can go first.) Talk about *your own* overall level of comfort with sexuality—how high or low it is. If your own level of comfort with sexuality is not as high as you'd like it to be, talk about things you think you could do to raise it, and how you think your partner might be able to help you in raising it.
5) Next, go on to sexual interest. Turn back to Figure 1 and think of it as showing a normal distribution for overall sexual *interest*. Take turns

pointing out exactly where you would put yourself along the horizontal axis. (Do *not* indicate where, along that axis, you think your partner is.) Then discuss whether you two are close enough in level of sexual interest, given where you placed yourselves, for it not to be a problem. If either of you thinks that you two are not close enough, then talk about what *you yourself* could do to make that difference less of a problem.

6) Now consider your sexual styles. Simultaneously show each other the hand rotations you did in response to the defining question about sexual style. Flip a coin to decide who talks first, and then—if it's possible for you—describe *your own* sexual style. Talk in terms of how you conceptualize sex; what sex is *primarily* for you. And, if you can, describe the kind of identity you want to take on, the kind of person you most want to be, during sex. Then if you don't think your sexual style meshes as well as you'd like with your partner's, talk about what *you* might be willing to try to get your styles to mesh better.

7) When you and your partner have finished your dialogue, and you're by yourself again, focus in on that last defining question, for the Sexual Dimension as a whole, get a felt sense, and express it to yourself with your hands. If you have read *Focusing* and learned to do all six focusing movements, then do a full focusing session on the felt sense that you just experienced.

I know how very hard it can be to go through this dialogue on the Sexual Dimension. You may well not be able to do it right now. But if you and your partner can manage to do it sometime before you get married, you will be way ahead.

11

THE WAVELENGTH
DIMENSION

Similarity on the Wavelength Dimension is the key to having a marriage in which you feel emotionally intimate with your partner and feel that your partner is truly your *companion*. As I've mentioned earlier, it's possible for people to have an intimate and happy marriage if they disagree on the Practical Dimension, and sometimes even if they don't have a very good sex life, as long as they are close on the Wavelength Dimension. If partners are close on the other two dimensions but not on the same wavelength, they can have a marriage that is workable and satisfying, a marriage that can last and that will be fulfilling in many ways—but they'll always have a sense that something's missing. They may not be able to say exactly what it is, but they'll feel it: They'll feel the lack of that sense of close communion, of oneness, that partners can have only if they are on the same wavelength.

When I introduced the Wavelength Dimension in chapter 2, I suggested that it could be summed up in the question "If my partner were of the same sex as I, would they be one of my very best friends?" And I pointed out that our very best friends are the people who *get it* when we talk to them. They instantly understand what we mean and they affirm it.

Let's take a closer look at that experience of being best friends and see what it's made of. Once you have a clear idea of that, you'll be able to determine how close you and your partner are on the Wavelength Dimension.

"We Can Talk About Everything"

Imagine a typical day in your life. Imagine that it's summer and it's hot outside. It's been hot for the past two weeks. It was already hot when you woke up. It was hot getting to work. It was so hot that just walking from the train station or the parking lot you sweated through your clothes. You enter the building where you work, feel the chill blast of the air-conditioning, sigh with relief, and press the button for the elevator. While you're waiting for the elevator, you notice that someone else is waiting. You look at him and instantly recognize, just from how he looks, that he is very different from you; you two probably have nothing in common. But you notice that this other person has also sweated through his clothes. Suddenly, this other person catches your eye and says, "Hot enough for ya?" You chuckle and say, "Tell me about it."

In that brief interchange, you and this other person had a moment of *empathy*. That is, each of you *knew what it felt like* to be the other—to feel the heat and to suffer from it. You two might not be able to find anything else to talk about nor understand each other in a deep way. But you could do it about the weather. In this one respect, if in no other, your lived experience coincided with the lived experience of this other person. That's why, when we meet up with a stranger, we talk about the weather. We know that we can have a moment of empathy with anybody if we talk about the weather because it's the one thing we all have in common.

Back to your day. A few hours after your encounter by the elevator, you go out to lunch with a few of your coworkers. They're nice people and you like them. Over lunch you and they discuss a TV show that you all watched the night before, a sitcom. Your coworkers talk about the parts they thought were funny and the parts they thought were stupid. Mostly, you agree with what they are saying; you empathize with them. Sometimes, they say something about the show that you think is off the wall. You might tell them that you don't agree with them, or even that they're off the wall. But then again you might say to yourself, "That's just them. It wouldn't hurt their feelings if I told them why they're off the wall, but why bother—they wouldn't get it anyway. They're them and I'm me."

You have enough in common with your coworkers—your lived experience coincides with theirs at enough points—so you can talk with them about many things and feel empathy. You can talk not only about TV shows but about clothes, sports, vacations, cars, computers, even some items in the news. You can talk with your coworkers about almost anything—*as long as you keep it light*. You know that you can't talk with them about anything heavy. From your conversations with them about light topics, you know that if you tried to talk with them about your hopes and dreams, your frustrations and disappointments, your deepest convictions about what's right and wrong, worthy and unworthy, it wouldn't work. You would feel awkward and so would they; and likewise, if they tried to talk with you about these heavy topics. Neither they nor you would understand what the other was trying to say, and you wouldn't know how to respond to one another. There would never be that feeling of empathy. Your lived experience doesn't coincide enough with theirs for you to feel empathy with one another at that deep and serious level. So you and your coworkers keep it light, empathize with one another at that light level, and have a good time together doing it. But you keep it at that.

Back again to your day. After work lets out, you meet one of your very best friends for pizza and a couple of beers. You two might talk about last night's sitcom, and have some laughs doing it. But you might skip the sitcom because you have more important things to talk about: the heavy stuff. When you and your friend talk about the heavy stuff, neither of you has to edit yourself. You can just be yourselves and let it all hang out. You each know that the other one will understand and will respond in ways that are interesting and helpful. Many things your friend says back to you might have never occurred to you. But they're things that relate to *your own understanding* of what you're talking about. When you and this very best friend of yours talk about the heavy stuff, each of you knows what it feels like to be the other. You each recognize something of yourself in the other. You have empathy at that deep, heavy level.

This is what people mean when they say, "We can talk about everything." By "everything" they don't mean literally everything under the sun—they mean the heavy stuff, the personally important subjects that they can't talk about with anyone except their very best friends, because only their very best friends will understand.

You can use this idea, "We can talk about everything," to get a sense of how close you and your partner are on the Wavelength Dimension. Think about the various people you have conversations with: your family, coworkers, friends, very best friends—your partner. Replay the film clips of those conversations in your imagination. Get a sense of how the conversations you have with some of these people feel different from the conversations you have with the others. Get a sense of what it feels like for you to experience empathy with your very best friends when you talk to them about the heavy stuff that you can't discuss with most people. Then answer the next defining question.

—How close do you and your partner come to being able to *talk about everything*?

"We Look at Things the Same Way"

Now back to you and this very best friend of yours. If someone came up to you and asked, "What makes it possible for you two to talk about everything?" you might reply, "We look at things the same way." Or you might use a variety of phrases that point to pretty much the same thing: "We react the same way," "Our outlooks are similar," "We have similar attitudes," "We share many of the same beliefs," or simply, "We have a lot in common."

Let me suggest another phrase, one that sums up all these other phrases and gets at exactly what it is that you and your very best friend have in common: *your personal truth.*

Your Personal Truth

When I say "your personal truth," I don't mean "truth" in its most common, everyday sense: when we use it to mean that some claim agrees with the facts, as in, "The truth is I have a younger sister, not a younger brother as you just said I did." The sense of truth I'm talking about is the sense we mean when we say about something, "Ain't it the truth," versus saying, "That's ridiculous!" (or "nonsense," "baloney," "bull," etc.). When we use "truth" in this way, what we mean is that some story we just heard agrees with how we think things *really are* out there in the world. The story agrees with how *we personally* make sense out of things.

We make sense of the events that we see out there in the world by making up our own stories about them. This applies equally to events that happen to other people and events that happen to us. The stories aren't out there in the world; all that's out there are events, which are neutral. *We* make up the stories. And while the events are neutral, the stories we make up about them all have a *moral*—a claim about how things *really are*. This hypothetical example will show you what I mean:

A man walking down a busy sidewalk in a big city slips on a banana peel and lands right on his butt. That's the event. Two other people walking down that same sidewalk, Chuck and George, witness this event. The story that Chuck makes up for it is "That guy wasn't watching where he was going. His head was in the clouds somewhere and so he slipped, just like in the cartoons." The moral that Chuck draws from his story is "It's a jungle out there. You'd better take care of yourself or else you'll end up on your butt, just like that poor slob did." George's story for the same event is different: "Some jerk was stupid enough and inconsiderate enough to drop a banana peel on a crowded sidewalk where it was a sure bet that somebody would slip on it." The moral that George draws from his story is "Jerks like the one who dropped that banana peel are a menace to the rest of us, no matter how careful we try to be. Today it was this guy's turn, tomorrow it could be mine."

Because their stories for the same event are so different, Chuck and George react differently. Chuck reacts with amusement. He shakes his head, laughs slightly, and he walks on by. George doesn't laugh when he sees the man slip on the banana peel. It's not funny to him. All he feels is anger and outrage—he'd love to get his hands on the guy who dropped that banana peel—and he feels compassion for the man who slipped on it. George goes over to him and helps him get back on his feet.

Same event—two different stories, two different emotional reactions, two different behavioral reactions. Two different personal truths.

Experiencing Your Personal Truth: The Michael Eisner Story

You can sample your own personal truth right now by reading about an event that actually happened.

On December 4, 1997, Michael D. Eisner, chairman and CEO of the Walt Disney Corporation, exercised some of his stock options. Stock options are a fringe benefit that corporations give to their high-ranking executives. An option is the right to buy a share of the company's stock at a price much lower than its current market price. As soon as the executive exercises the option (usually options, for many shares of stock) and purchases the shares, he realizes a substantial profit (on paper, at least). If he then turns around and sells those shares at the current market price, that substantial profit is transformed from a paper profit to real money. Please note that making money from options is perfectly legitimate; people do it all the time.

What Michael Eisner did on December 4, 1997, was exercise options for 7.3 million shares of Disney stock. The price of one share of Disney stock that morning was about $95. Mr. Eisner's options allowed him to purchase most of the 7.3 million shares for $17.14 and some of them for $19.64. The instant Mr. Eisner acquired the 7.3 million shares of Disney stock he realized a profit, on paper, of $565 million. He then sold 4 million of those shares at the current market price and made a pretax, real-money profit of $374 million. After taxes, Mr. Eisner ended up with a net profit of about $131 million out of the $374 million.[1]

THAT'S THE EVENT. To discover your personal truth about it, start with your feelings. What was the main feeling you experienced reading the story? It could have been anything: excitement, encouragement, envy. Those are just three examples of the countless ways someone could have felt reading about that event.

Once you've determined what your main feeling was, you can work backward from there to the moral of your story about the event, and then back to the story itself. If your main feeling was excitement or encouragement, the moral of your story may have been "If people are smart and work hard, the sky's the limit. I'm smart, I work hard. That could be me someday." The story from which you drew that moral might then be "Michael Eisner was smart, played his cards right and worked hard—and so he got rewarded accordingly." If your main feeling was envy, the moral of your story may have been "Some people are lucky, that's all." Your story itself might have gone something like "Michael Eisner may be smart and he may work hard, but lots of people are smart and work hard, and they'd need thousands of lifetimes to make what he made in one day. He happened to be at the right place at the right time. He was probably *born* at the right place at the right time. And he must have had the right combination of breaks every step of the way. I don't have that kind of luck."

Same event, different personal truths. Every day as you watch the events around you, and react to them, you react the way you do because of your personal truth about those events. The stories you make up about events and the morals you draw are what your personal truth is made of.

Your personal truth determines your reactions not just to raw events but also to other people's *stories* about events. If someone else's story jibes with your own personal truth, you buy their story. That is, your reaction to the moral of their story is "Ain't it the truth. That's the way things *really are*." If their story doesn't jibe with your personal truth, you don't buy it. We're all bombarded, all the time, with other people's stories—not just the stories other people tell to us personally, but the stories we're presented with in books and magazines, on television and in movies. For example, take (you guessed it) *Elvira Madigan*. The makers of that movie were pitching a moral that would go something like this: "Passionate love is often tragic. This is not the fault of the lovers because they can't help loving each other. It's the fault of a cruel, unfeeling society that won't understand their love." That moral jibed with Jennifer's personal truth about love, so the movie touched her deeply. It didn't jibe with my personal truth, so the movie left me cold.

The things experts tell us—politicians, teachers, preachers, psychotherapists—in their speeches, lessons, sermons, and self-help books are also stories. These experts are all trying to convince us that something *really is* as they say it is, and they're all hoping we'll respond with "Ain't it the truth."

There's no way to briefly describe or summarize your personal truth—say, by listing your background, beliefs, attitudes, IQ, and personality traits. That's because all these aspects of you, and many others, interact in complicated ways to form your personal truth. Also, your personal truth emerges only piece by piece, as you make sense of the infinite variety of events and stories you're exposed to day after day. There's no way to briefly summarize all that.

It doesn't matter that you can't fully describe or explain your personal truth. What does matter is that your personal truth is always at work in determining your reactions to everything around you. So when you say things like "We see things the same way," "We react the same way," "We have the same attitudes and beliefs," you're pointing to the fact that your personal truth closely matches the personal truth of someone else. In other words, *when you and someone else are on the same wavelength, your personal truth matches up closely with theirs.*

The idea of personal truth gives you another perspective from which to view how close you and your partner are on the Wavelength Dimension. So now, based on your experience of comparing your reactions and your partner's to the events and stories that are presented to you every day, answer this next defining question.

—How closely does your personal truth match up with your partner's personal truth?

"We Agree on the Important Things"

In response to that inquisitive person's question about what made you and another person very best friends, you might also have said, "We agree on the important things." This is certainly something that happily married couples say when they try to explain why they're happy. Notice that they don't say they agree on everything—just on the important things.

What is important? The first important thing that best friends and happily married people agree on is . . . what's important. Now, that doesn't mean that all the exact same things are equally important to each of them (although I'd imagine that there would be quite a few things that would be equally important). It does mean that each partner feels that the things the other partner regards as important are worthy of being regarded as

important—*even if those particular things are not important to him or her.*
Music is important to me and it's not important to Sue. But Sue thinks it's
perfectly reasonable that I'd spend an hour listening to the same thirty-
second Charlie Parker solo over and over again.[2] Likewise, I think it's
perfectly legitimate for Sue to want to stand in front of one of her
favorite paintings for a length of time that would bore me to sleep or
cause me to faint (whichever came first). By contrast, think back to Paul
and Justine, the couple with the arranged marriage in chapter 2. Paul
couldn't fathom how soap operas could be so important to Justine, and
Justine couldn't fathom how current events could be so important to
Paul. They didn't agree that what was important to their partner was
worthy of being regarded as important.

The Big Issues

Happily married couples also agree on what I call the Big Issues. The
Big Issues are the things that are important and inescapable for all of us.
They have this importance because we inevitably have to deal with them
in deciding how to live our lives. The Big Issues are values and aspira-
tions, sense of justice, and spiritual orientation. Agreeing on those Big
Issues is a large part of agreeing on the important things.

VALUES AND ASPIRATIONS. I've grouped values and aspirations
together because our aspirations are a natural outgrowth of our values.
For example, if power is something you value highly, you might aspire to
be a politician or a high-ranking corporate executive. If being rich, but
not necessarily powerful, is what you value highly, you might aspire to
be a commodities trader. If being close to nature is what you value most
highly, you might aspire to be a marine biologist like Jacques Cousteau,
or a forest ranger. You wouldn't want to be a forest ranger if your highest value is being rich, or a currency trader if your highest value is being
close to nature. Our values and aspirations, in that sense, are inseparable.

Identifying your values: what you want *most*. There are several
different methods you can use to get a better idea of what your values
really are. One way is to ask yourself these three questions about your life:

1) In my life, what do I *most* want to *be?*
2) In my life, what do I *most* want to *do?*
3) In my life, what do I *most* want to *have?*

Notice that the word "most" is emphasized in these questions. That's because when you're trying to identify your values, it's not simply a matter of listing what's important to you. What you have to do is decide what's *more* important than what, and ultimately what's *most* important. The list of what's important to you would probably be very long; each of us considers many things to be important. That long list, though, probably wouldn't give you, or anyone else looking at it, much of an idea of exactly how you intended to direct your life. By contrast, your list of what is *most* important to you, once you'd gone through the process of deciding what's more important than what, would be relatively short. And that short list would convey a good idea of how you intended to direct your life.

For example, if you put a gun to my head, attached me to a polygraph to make sure I was telling the truth, and then said to me, "OK, Sam, answer those three questions—and use no more than two items to answer each one," my answers would be: (1) In my life, I most want to be *a good craftsman* in my work as a psychotherapist and a *good father*; (2) What I most want to do is *what little I can to reduce the sum total of suffering in the world*; (3) What I most want to have is *more knowledge and understanding in general (and of music in particular)* and *more free time.*

I invite you to pose these three questions to yourself. Determine what your answers are. Then think about what your partner's answers might be.

One caution about determining what you most value using this method and also the ones that follow: You don't have to try to understand *why* you value what you do or question whether your values are worthy. The reasons you value what you do are varied and complex. You may be aware of some of them; you're probably not aware of many of them. And right now, the point is to identify *what* your values are, not why; to identify them, not judge them. I do think that it's a good idea for us to question our values all the time, but for you, right now, all that's necessary is that you know what they are.

Identifying your values: trade-offs. Another way to get a clearer idea of your values is to think about which trade-offs you're willing to make, and which trade-offs you're not willing to make. It's become a cliché, by now, that you can't have it all and that life is a matter of trade-offs. But there is truth to clichés, and it is illuminating to look at your values in the light of trade-offs. The following list of questions includes some of the major trade-offs that life presents to us:

> —If you had to choose between a job that was not interesting at all but was high paying and a job that was very interesting but didn't pay nearly as well, which one would you choose?
> —Likewise, how about the choice between a job that was not very secure but allowed a lot of personal freedom versus a job that was very secure but didn't allow a great deal of personal freedom?
> —Would you be likely to accept a job that was a fabulous career opportunity but required you to spend a great deal of time away from your partner (and children) for three or four years—either because the job required very long working hours or because it required a lot of travel?

People are called upon to decide on these sorts of trade-offs all the time: people who join high-powered law firms, people who go into medical residency training, people who decide to stick with corporate life instead of venturing out on their own, people who do decide to venture out on their own.

You may have already had to make some decisions about trade-offs yourself. Which way did you go? Which way did your partner go? If you had to make similar trade-off decisions, did you both go the same way? You can think about all of these questions to get a clearer idea of your values and of your partner's.

Identifying your values: ambition. To get yet another perspective on your values, you can take the direct approach. That is, you can round up the usual suspects—money, power, achievement, fame—and ask yourself how important each of these is to you. In a word, you can ask yourself, "How *ambitious* am I?"

In answering the part of the question that's about money, don't think in terms of numbers. Instead, think in terms of this sentence, "I want enough money to _____." Then fill in the blank whichever way you want, as many times as you want: "send my kids to the expensive private college of their choice," "retire by the time I'm forty," "feel financially secure so I don't have to worry about money all the time, the way I do now," "have vacation homes in the Virgin Islands and the south of France"—whatever. When you think about fame, power, and achievement, think about whichever person best represents each of these to you, and ask yourself if living his or her life would appeal to you.

As you consider your own level of ambition, please consider your partner's level of ambition as well, even if that's not something that's concerned you much up to now. Sooner or later it will. The story of Linda and Wes is an example of how a mismatch in expectations for your partner's ambition can sneak up on you and cause problems.

Linda's relationship with her father, Gordon, had been stormy all her life. Gordon was an immensely successful corporate lawyer—managing partner of a huge firm. He was a hard-driving Type A personality who was always working and could never slow down and relax. Worse, Gordon was as impatient, demanding, perfectionistic, and unrelenting with Linda as he was with the lawyers who worked for him. Linda felt oppressed by the way her father treated her throughout her childhood, and even up through college.

Sure enough, the man Linda fell in love with and married was nothing like her father. Wes was warm, understanding, tolerant, accepting, nondemanding, and altogether laid-back. In fact, he was so laid-back that he was not career-oriented at all. Wes did work, but at a low-paying job that was far below what would be expected of a person with his intelligence and education. He was happy, though, right where he was. Linda wasn't. She resented that she had to work as hard as she did, and that it was she who had to earn the lion's share of the money they needed to maintain their lifestyle. Linda came to realize that, in marrying Wes, she had thrown out the baby with the bathwater. She realized that, although she didn't want a husband who was impatient, demanding, and perfectionistic, as her father was, she *did* want a man who was career-oriented and ambitious—someone just like her father, at least in those respects.

IDENTIFYING YOUR VALUES: THE FANTASY METHOD. One final way you can identify your values is by the fantasy method. This fantasy is one I bet you've entertained more than once—most people have—but not to clarify your values: What would you do if you won one of those megajackpots in the lottery—$20 million or more, let's say? How, for example, would you spend the first $100,000? Would you buy a yacht, give it to your widowed mother, or what? And then what would you do with the rest? For argument's sake, let's assume you're about thirty-five years old at the time, so that you're reasonably well along on whatever career path you've chosen. You win $20 million. How much about your life do you change—everything, almost nothing at all?

Most of the time, when we entertain this fantasy, we don't play it out all the way. We simply imagine a couple of things we'd really like ("I'll buy a home in Aspen and spend all my time skiing and golfing") and leave it at that. But $20 million is a lot of money, and if you win it at age thirty-five you have a lot of time left in which to spend it. So how, exactly, would you live your life all those years after you struck it rich? Spin out the whole story. What do you think your partner's story would be?

Once you've looked at your values and aspirations from the different perspectives I've described, you're in a position to answer this next defining question:

—How closely do your values and aspirations agree with those of your partner?

SENSE OF JUSTICE. By your "sense of justice," I simply mean your attitudes on political and social issues. Justice—what's fair and what isn't—is what all political and social questions boil down to. If you are in favor of affirmative action, that's because you think it is fair to African-Americans and women and not unfair to white men. If you are against affirmative action, that's because you think it is unfair to white men. If you think the tax system should be changed in some way, that's because you think the tax system is unfair. If you think the criminal justice system should be changed somehow, that's because you think it's unfair—whether to criminals or to victims. And so on, down the line. So, when you think about how you and your partner respond to political and social questions, I'd like you to think in terms of fairness—of justice.

Now, you may be doubtful that your sense of justice could affect the quality of your romantic relationship or your marriage. But it can, and it often does. A while ago, I talked to a former client of mine whom I hadn't spoken with in a couple of years. He is a very good-natured, tolerant man. I recalled a serious relationship he'd been involved in when we'd last talked, and I asked him about it: "So, Blake, whatever happened with you and that high-powered insurance executive you were going out with?" He replied, "Well, Sam, you know that I'm a conservative Republican. Tanya is a liberal Democrat. I liked [President] Bush, she hated him. When we'd see something on the news about welfare mothers, or walk down the street and see a panhandler, she'd have one take on it and I'd have another. We'd get into terrible fights. It just didn't work out."

Your sense of justice affects your marriage also because it influences practical decisions you make about how to live. For example, it affects what kind of neighborhood you decide to move into, and what school you decide is best for your kids. Couples even decide to move from one state to another because they feel the political climate in the new state matches their sense of justice better than the political climate in the old state did.

I don't have to give you an exhaustive list of the issues you respond to through your sense of justice. You certainly know what the big ones are: race, jobs, wages, taxes, abortion, immigration, poverty, welfare, crime. So think back, now, on the times you and your partner have discussed these sorts of issues. Recall how comfortable you felt in those discussions. Did you feel you could express your opinions freely, or did you hold back because you expected that your partner would disagree? Did you two, in fact, mostly agree or did you mostly disagree? When you disagreed, how heated were those disagreements, how bad did they feel for you? Once you've thought back on all that, and gotten a felt sense, you can answer the next defining question:

—How closely does your partner's sense of justice agree with your own?

SPIRITUAL ORIENTATION. Your spiritual orientation doesn't consist only of your attitudes toward religion. It also consists of your bedrock beliefs about what kind of world it is that we all live in, and why things happen in the way they do.

Your attitudes about religion are the place to start, though, in thinking about your spiritual orientation. First of all, do you consider yourself a member of an organized religion? If that religion is not the one you were born into, by what path did you end up there? Do you believe in God, in the way that God is described in your religion? Sometimes people don't. For example, Albert Einstein identified himself as a Jew and as a spiritual person, but he didn't believe in a God who parted the Red Sea for the children of Israel, or who otherwise intervenes in history and in our individual lives. Sometimes people who are not sure about whether there is a God practice their religion anyway, because they find the practice itself to be important. Speaking of religious practice, how fulfilling and enriching do you find it? What part does prayer play in your life?

Beliefs about religious observance and practice are very individual and very deeply held; it wouldn't be surprising if you and your partner differed on these beliefs in some ways. Couples can bridge differences on religion, even large ones, provided that they can appreciate how deeply held each other's beliefs are. Vincent and Camille both grew up in the same religious tradition. Their difference was that while Camille did believe in God and value their religious tradition, Vincent was a thoroughgoing atheist who had no use for any organized religion. Luckily, they were so close on the Wavelength Dimension in other respects (and on the other two compatibility dimensions as well), and they respected each other so highly, that each allowed the other to do what he or she wanted about religion. Their children were given religious training because Camille very much wanted that and Vincent didn't care one way or the other. Of course, not all couples are able to attain the level of mutual tolerance that Vincent and Camille did; and if there are significant religious differences between you and your partner, you will have to carefully consider what level of tolerance you two will be able to achieve.

I guess this is the point where I have to say a few words about inter-faith marriage. It won't be more than a few words because I'm not an expert on interfaith marriage, and because you can read good books about it written by people who are experts. If you read these books, you'll see that there are many different ways to have a successful interfaith mar-riage; you just have to find the way that works for you. In my view, inter-faith issues are a problem only for couples who haven't realized that getting married means transferring their primary loyalty away from their families of origin to the new family they've created by getting married. For those couples, intrusive, disapproving family members can cause dis-sension, confusion, and havoc. It won't be that way for you if you are mindful of transferring your primary loyalty to the new family you're creating. (You will probably have to transfer that primary loyalty to each other long before you get married, since "what kind of wedding to have" can be one of the most toxic interfaith issues.)

Your spiritual orientation, though, is far more than your attitudes toward religion. Most fundamentally, your spiritual orientation has to do with your beliefs about *why* the world is as it is. In his final delirium, my father, who would die of his cancer just a few days later, wept through his closed eyes and whispered, over and over again, "Why?" "Why did they kill my mother?" "Why did they kill my brothers?" "Why did they kill my sister?" My father's brothers and sister, children at the time, and his mother had been murdered by the Nazis more than forty-five years before—and still, on his deathbed, he was asking, "Why?"

"Why?" is the question we ask ourselves about so many things, not just genocide. If we have religious faith we ask the overarching question posed by the Book of Job: "If God is good, why is there evil in the world?" If we haven't religious faith, we simply ask, "Why is there evil in the world?" And we ask why the evil that befalls people seems to be so unevenly distributed. Why are some particular children born with horri-ble birth defects and not other particular children? Why did *that* airplane fall from the sky, and not the plane I flew on yesterday? Do things happen for reasons, or do they just happen? And if they happen for reasons, what are the reasons? Are they reasons that we can know or reasons that will always be a mystery to us? Is what happens in the world—including the very fact that we exist—all part of some ordered plan, even if we can never understand the order of that plan, or is there no plan? Do things eventually turn out for the best or don't they? Is there hope or is there no hope?

Your answers to "Why?" and the other questions that derive from it are the heart of your spiritual orientation. This is so whether your answers are faith-based or not. Even if you consider yourself an atheist, you have some kind of spiritual orientation, and your answers to these questions are it.

When partners differ in their characteristic answers to "Why?" it can be a frustrating experience for both. Virginia and Dexter both believed in God, but had different views of God's role in the destiny of individual human beings. Whenever they heard about something bad that happened—whether to strangers or to someone they knew— Virginia's response was "Things happen for reasons." This exasperated Dexter, who could never see any good "reasons" for tragedies, and he accused Virginia of using her belief as a way of protecting herself against the feelings of terror and grief that tragedies produce. What Dexter regarded as realism, Virginia regarded as cynicism; and when it was directed at her it hurt terribly.

You have a sense of your spiritual orientation because you've asked "Why?" many times and you know what kinds of answers you've given yourself. You may not be able to state your spiritual orientation coherently—that's a hard thing for some of us to do—but you have a felt sense of what it is.

By now, you certainly know what your partner's orientation is toward religious observance and practice. You may also have a good idea about what kinds of answers your partner gives to the "Why?" questions. In case you don't, it's easy to find out. Just ask. It won't be hard to find something specific to talk about; fresh disasters and atrocities are served up to us every day on the evening news. Once you and your partner have talked about "Why?" you'll be able to answer the next defining question.

—To what degree do you and your partner share the same spiritual orientation?

Now it's time for you to get a felt sense of how closely you and your partner agree on the important things. Reflect back on the degree to which you and your partner agree on what's important, and the degree of closeness you feel with your partner on each of the Big Issues. Put it all together and focus in.

—To what degree do you and your partner agree on the important things?

"We Want the Same Things"

This is also something that people say when describing their relationship with their very best friends. It is certainly something that couples say when they are on the same wavelength. Happily married couples mean two different things when they say "We want the same things." The first thing they mean is that they share the same values and aspirations. They also mean something related to that, but larger: *They mean that they want to live the same kind of life.* Whether it's life in the fast lane or in the slow lane, whether it's a life centered around fame and fortune or around communion with nature, there are some *particular* things that both partners care about most. These special things provide the couple with the unique, underlying themes for their life together. I call these special, theme-creating things *primary concerns.*

The best way for you to immediately see what I mean by "primary concerns" is to hear someone describe his primary concern. This is Jon Krakauer, in his gripping book about the 1996 Mount Everest disaster, *Into Thin Air:*

> By the time I was in my early twenties climbing had become the focus of my existence to the exclusion of almost anything else. Achieving the summit of a mountain was tangible, immutable, concrete. The incumbent hazards lent the activity a seriousness of purpose that was sorely missing from the rest of my life. . . . In those years I lived to climb, existing on five or six thousand dollars a year, working as a carpenter and a commercial salmon

fisherman just long enough to fund the next trip to the Bugaboos or Tetons or Alaska range. [pp. 20–21]

A primary concern is more than just an interest you have. It is not just something that's important to you. A primary concern is something that is essential to your *being* you; something that, if it were somehow removed from you, you wouldn't be you. It is something your life revolves around, something that gives your life meaning and direction, something your life is about. It is what *you* are about.

The primary concerns that you and your partner share can be anything at all: an interest or activity, your work, a goal, or an ideal. Here's a sampling of primary concerns that are shared by some happily married couples I know.

Recovery is a primary concern that Jackie and Roy share. They both have been in the AA program for many years, and they devote a great deal of time and attention to "working the program" so that they can maintain and strengthen their sobriety. And, in accordance with AA's Twelfth Step, they also devote a lot of energy to helping people who are just starting out in AA.

Dogs are the primary concern for Owen and Elaine. They are both schoolteachers, a profession they chose, in part, because it allows them abundant free time to devote to their collies. Owen and Elaine breed collies and sell some of them, but they aren't in it for the money. They simply love breeding, training, and showing dogs. It is their life. (If you have one dog, you know how much time that takes. Now think about six or eight, including newborn puppies.) On school holidays and for the entire summer Owen and Elaine pack themselves and their dogs into their RV and drive to dog shows all over the country.

Sailing is one of the primary concerns that Fran and Bob share. Whenever they're not working, they're on the boat. Sailing played a very important part in the upbringing of their two sons. It was a main way they all experienced family togetherness. After the boys left home for college, Fran and Bob moved to the Jersey shore so that they could be as close to the ocean and their boat as possible.

Being of service is a primary concern that Debbie and Paul share.

For a number of years Paul was minister to a congregation in a wealthy suburb—until he decided that there wasn't enough ministering for him to do there. He asked the governing board of his denomination for a transfer to someplace where he could really be of service. They obliged him: Paul and Debbie moved to a remote community fifteen hundred miles away, where Paul was given the challenge of starting a new congregation—at a salary far less than the one he had enjoyed in his former position. Paul worked hard, loved it, and succeeded not only in organizing a new congregation but also in raising the money to build a new church facility for it. Meanwhile, Debbie became actively involved in the community's battered women's shelter.

Craftsmanship is one of the primary concerns that Gene and Mary Alice share. Doing a careful, thorough, craftsmanlike job is Gene's central focus no matter what he's doing, whether it's making meticulously accurate drawings of archaeological artifacts, designing museum exhibits, rebuilding his front steps, or even cleaning a coffeepot. Mary Alice is an art historian and curator. Whether she's trying to figure out the painter of an unsigned painting, or the exact date of a Colonial-era portrait, there is the same concern for craftsmanship. For Mary Alice, that craftsmanship consists of being meticulous in her research—locating every document, cross-checking every fact, so that she always gets it exactly right.

Being a doctor has been the primary concern of my oldest friend, Josh, ever since we first met, when he was six and I was seven. It wasn't the money part of being a doctor that motivated Josh. It wasn't exactly the helping others part either. What most appealed to Josh was the idea that doctors have the ability—the power—to cure people in amazing ways. Josh became the kind of doctor where that ability is most clear-cut (so to speak)—a surgeon. Josh has devoted his adult life, day and night, to being a doctor. So has Josh's wife, Carol, who is also a doctor.

Justice for all is a primary concern that Sherry and Mike share. They both graduated from top law schools and could have written their own ticket. They became public defenders instead. And their son is named after one of their favorite Supreme Court justices.

The outdoors is a primary concern that Louisa and Martin share. Just about every weekend, whether the temperature is 100 above or 20 below, they're outside: hiking, snowshoeing, backpacking—anything as long as it's out in the wilderness. They met on the trail, of course.

Building our dream house was the shared primary concern of Ruby and Danny for many years. They designed it together, picked the furnishings together, and even did a great deal of the actual building of it together.

These are just a few examples of the primary concerns that couples can share. Many couples, though, share only one primary concern: *our children*. That one shared primary concern often is enough to provide them with a shared focus and a shared way for imagining and structuring their future. Sometimes it isn't enough, and the partners start wondering just what, aside from the kids, they're getting out of their marriage.

When a couple shares no primary concerns, or only "our children," they can still have a stable and functioning marriage. But if their *unshared* primary concerns are very different, the couple will be pulled apart by them, and may even break up over them. Here's an example: Erica and Henry were both painters, and met in art school. They were realistic enough to realize that they wouldn't be able to eat if they tried to support themselves as painters, so they got degrees in art education. They figured that with teaching positions they'd be able to survive and still pursue their art. Erica got a job at a small college in New England, and Henry got a job at a boarding school nearby—and they moved from the city to the country. Country life suited Henry just fine. He enjoyed working on the old stone farmhouse they lived in, and he even started raising a few chickens. Erica did not take to country life, which she felt was claustrophobic. More important, she realized that although she could indeed paint in the country, she needed to be "in the art world"—and she needed to succeed in that world. This was her primary concern, one that Henry didn't share—and it was enough to motivate her to leave him and move back to the city.

When you and your partner do have shared primary concerns, they are a vehicle for you to feel emotional intimacy with each other, and to feel a sense of uniqueness and specialness about that intimacy. Chances are that if you've felt close with your partner on the Wavelength Dimension, in the ways I described earlier in this chapter—especially if your values and aspirations and your spiritual orientations closely match—you

will have some shared primary concerns. But now it's time for you to
address that question directly.

—Do you and your partner have some shared primary concerns?

As we've gone through the Wavelength Dimension, I've asked you to
think about it in terms of your relationship with your very best friend.
When you and your partner are on the same wavelength, that's what you
are—very best friends.

We've looked at that relationship from several different perspectives:
empathy, personal truth, shared values, sense of justice, spiritual orientation, and primary concerns. Now it's time for you to get a sense of how
close you and your partner are on the Wavelength Dimension all
together. So think about your experience of reading this chapter. (You
may want to read the chapter over again, because although it's not that
long, there's a lot in it.) Recall how close you felt to your partner when
you looked at the Wavelength Dimension from each of the different perspectives. Focus in and get a felt sense of all that.

—How close are you and your partner on the Wavelength Dimension?

Dialogue

Now it's time for you and your partner to talk with each other about your
felt sense of closeness on the Wavelength Dimension:

1) Find a quiet place where you can sit across from each other at a table.
2) Simultaneously show each other your hand rotation for that last
   defining question, on the Wavelength Dimension as a whole.
3) Each of you translate your hand rotation into words, using just a sentence or two—for example, "I feel wonderfully close to you on this

dimension and I think we'll really be able to affirm each other on it," or "I'm just a little nervous about it. We'll have some problems about it, but I think we'll be OK," or "I'm really worried about it. I think it will be hard for us to affirm each other on this dimension."

4) Take turns in bringing up an aspect of the dimension that's of particular concern to you. Describe the experiences you two have had on it that cause you concern. Describe how you think your differences on it might affect your marriage. Describe what would have to be different about you, your partner, and your relationship so that you would not be as concerned with that aspect of the dimension. Take as many turns as you need to bring up all your concerns.

5) Go through the chapter together and mention anything—positive as well as negative—that occurred to you when you went through the chapter individually.

6) When you and your partner have finished your dialogue and you're by yourself again, focus in on that last defining question, on the Wavelength Dimension as a whole, get a felt sense, and express it to yourself with your hands. If you have read *Focusing* and learned to do all six focusing movements, then do a full focusing session on the felt sense that you just experienced.

12

YIKES! WHAT DO WE DO NOW? AND YOUR (MY) OTHER QUESTIONS ANSWERED

Same deal here as in chapter 6: I've made up some questions to cover some points that were not discussed in enough detail, or were missed altogether, earlier in Part II. But I also suspect that, after having worked through the last three chapters and evaluated your compatibility with your partner, you may have some specific questions about what decisions to make. Once more, I hope that at least some of my questions match yours.

1. Yikes! What do we do now?

You may not even be asking this question because you've been working through this book by yourself, without a partner. And now you do know what to do the next time you become involved with someone. Or you have been working through the book with a partner, and everything came up roses for you: very close on all three dimensions. Good for you.

On the other hand, maybe you and your partner read the book carefully, considered each of the defining questions thoroughly, focused in deeply on how close you are on each of the dimensions—you even went out and rented *Elvira Madigan*—but you're still confused and unsure about how close you actually are on them. You believe, for instance, that you're reasonably close on them, but you're not sure if you're close enough. And so you wonder whether you should go ahead and become more committed to the relationship, or hold back on commitment for a while, or just call it quits. It's OK. Sit back, take a deep breath, relax, and we'll sort it all out.

2. How close is "close" and how far apart is "far apart" anyway?

Recall when I talked about different kinds of marriages, I talked about a *threshold* for feeling compatible. I compared it with the threshold for hearing: that point in the loudness of a sound where you just begin to hear it. In thinking about how close or far apart you are on any of the compatibility dimensions, you should think in terms of that threshold for feeling compatible. Focus in on the dimension, then say to yourself, "Yes, we are compatible enough," and see what felt sense comes up. If you get a good feeling in your body, then I would believe that you are compatible enough. If you get any kind of negative feeling in your body—a sense of tension in your neck, an increase in your heartbeat, a clutching feeling in your gut, anything like that—then I would doubt that you and your partner are close enough on that dimension to be compatible. Bear in mind that you *want* to feel close to your partner. So, if even in spite of that you don't feel close, that tells you a lot.

3. Can we use the final hand rotations we did for each dimension to tell us if we're compatible?

The Hand-Rotation Exercise is a way for you to express your felt sense of compatibility to yourself and to your partner. It does not give an objective, scientifically validated measure of how compatible you are. Consequently, you cannot simply measure the angles of your hand rotations to determine your compatibility. Much more important for determining your compatibility are the *qualitative* understandings that you and your partner gained from the dialogues that you did at the end of each of the previous three chapters.

That said, I can give you my *clinical impressions* of what kinds of hand rotations go with what kinds of couples. I don't think you'll be surprised by what I have to say. Happily married people with whom I've tried the exercise don't rotate their hands very much. Sometimes they don't rotate them at all; they just keep them congruent, with no angle between them. The largest rotation I've ever seen, in happy couples, is about 60 degrees, and that was for the Practical Dimension. I've never seen rotations nearly that large for the other two dimensions, in happy couples.

Troubled couples rotate their hands a lot, by which I mean more than 90 degrees. (Here, I am referring only to the Practical Dimension and the Wavelength Dimension. In my initial interview with couples, when I have them do the exercise, I do not use it to assess the sexual part of the relationship. Instead I do a historical survey, asking the partners to rate the quality of their sexual relationship—as excellent, good, fair, or poor—at different points in their life together.) It's not uncommon for troubled couples to display hand rotations on the other two dimensions that are closer to 180 degrees (hands pointing in opposite directions) than to 90 degrees (hands pointing perpendicular to each other). Another thing that happens in couples who have marital problems is that the two partners disagree on how compatible they are: One rotates their hands much more than the other. To me, that always means that the partners are not compatible—because it means they don't even perceive their relationship similarly.

Remember that the importance, to you, of any incompatibility between you and your partner will depend on what kind of marriage you want—or think you could be satisfied with. For example, let's say that you and your partner are close on the Practical Dimension and on the Sexual Dimension, but that you're not close on the Wavelength Dimension. If you think a two-dimensional, Practical/Sex marriage could work for you, as it seems to for some other couples, then that incompatibility on the Wavelength Dimension may not matter that much to you.

4. Isn't there some kind of test we can take, something that *will* give us a number for how compatible we are?

Yes, there is a test you can take, and it does yield a number—a set of numbers, as a matter of fact. But *you* don't get to see those numbers. The only one who gets to see them is the counselor who administered the test. The counselor then uses those numbers to guide you in a discussion of the "strength areas" (where you're compatible) and the "growth areas" (where you're not that compatible) in your relationship.

The test is called PREPARE.[1] It's a good test; I've used it myself. The test is high in what psychologists call *predictive validity*. That is, when the test has been given to large numbers of premarital couples, the scores have correctly predicted which couples would still be happily married (versus unhappily married, separated, or divorced), two or three years later, 80 to 85 percent of the time. You should be aware, though, that predictive validity, like other group-based statistical measures, cannot predict the outcome for any particular couple. That is, you and your partner may have scores that put you in the group where 85 percent of the couples stay together, but you may be one of the couples who don't; or your scores may predict that you'll break up, but you don't. Finally, you should bear in mind that PREPARE is only as good as the counselor who interprets it for you and then counsels you based on it. I encourage you to take PREPARE, if you at all want to. Just make sure in whatever way you can that the counselor you use is experienced enough and skilled enough to make the most of it for you.

My overall impression is that this book and PREPARE are complementary to each other. PREPARE gives *quantitative* information to *the counselor*. This book gives *qualitative* information to *you* so that you can counsel yourself, or assist a counselor in counseling you.

5. Are there things we can try to get closer on the compatibility dimensions?

Yes, there are. As I mentioned in chapter 10, you may be able to get closer on the Sexual Dimension simply by reading good books on sexuality together and learning to talk with each other about sex more openly and directly.

If you don't feel close enough on the Practical Dimension, there are a couple of things you can do—*provided that you do agree on your preferred model of marriage,* which is a must. The first thing you can do is anticipate where the problems will be, and then work out some deals on the issues that you expect will be conflictual. For example, let's say that you like to spend more time visiting with family than your partner does. In that case, you and your partner would work out a deal regarding how often, and for how much time per visit, your partner will join you. You two would also agree on exactly how you would talk with your family about your partner's not joining you sometimes. For working out these deals, good communication and problem-solving skills will naturally be a great advantage. (You can find good books on communication and problem solving listed in "For Further Reading," at the end of this book.)

The second thing you can do to get closer on the Practical Dimension is design and carry out some "HisWay/HerWay" experiments. I'll be explaining "HisWay/HerWay" experiments, and giving examples of them, in the next chapter.

As for the Wavelength Dimension, I don't know what to tell you. I believe that your wavelength is your wavelength. And as I said before, I think that when people change, over the course of the life cycle, the change is in the direction of becoming more purely and completely themselves.

Sometimes people can be confused about how close they are to their partner on the Wavelength Dimension because, although they are close on most aspects of it, they are far apart on one or two others. If that is the case with you, then in evaluating your overall closeness on the dimension you need to ask yourself how accepting you can be about the differences between you. Can you say, about your partner, "Well, that's just him [or her]," and really mean it? It's easier to mean it if the differences between you won't affect how you actually live your life. For example, I've met numbers of couples who, because of differences in their spiritual orientation or sense of justice, have opposing views on abortion. It's easier for these couples to agree to disagree if they know that they will never be faced with the decision of terminating a pregnancy.

If you and your partner are not close on the Wavelength Dimension, but still feel strongly that you want to be with each other, then what the two of you must do is actively imagine, together, what your relationship will be like, given this difference between you. As I've mentioned a couple of times before, you might find that you could have what you consider a good marriage, anyway.

6. Why didn't you discuss parenting as an issue on which partners can be more or less compatible?

I didn't because I believe that it's very hard to know how you feel about parenting, or what kind of parent you will be, until you've begun to experience what it's like to have a child. Until then, a lot of what you think about parenting is going to be awfully hypothetical. If you want to discuss parenting with each other, please do.

If one of you already has a child, or both of you do, then you already know what parenting is like, and you are in a position to compare your parenting styles and philosophies. You definitely should. On top of that, you've got to educate yourselves on the intricacies of stepparenting. "Blended family" issues are always tricky, and I couldn't begin to do justice to them in this book. Fortunately, there are some good books on these topics (again, see "For Further Reading" for one of them), and there are therapists who specialize in helping blended families.

7. What if we've gone through this book, taken PREPARE and done the counseling that goes along with that, *and we still don't know what to do?*

If you're having this much trouble deciding, I'm inclined to think that there's something important that's wrong, so my first recommendation would be: Get more counseling to figure out what that important something is.

Whether or not you elect to get counseling, it seems to me that you have to gather more information. That means giving your relationship more time. But that time period shouldn't be indefinite. You should specify a time frame by the end of which you will break up if you are as undecided then as you are now. When I encounter couples in this situation, I generally recommend a time period of between six and eighteen months—not longer.

8. What if we feel we've given our relationship plenty of time, and we feel we have to make a final decision *right now*?!?!?

I sympathize with you. Time *is* precious. And there does come a point when a couple who have been stuck have to make a final decision and then move on, either together or apart. If you have already given your relationship a lot of time, and if despite that you are still not wholehearted about getting married, I would urge caution. Remember that you *must* feel wholehearted about getting married, otherwise you ought not do it.

In extreme situations, where a couple have been stuck for a long time, and ask me for one last thing they can do before giving up, I have occasionally recommended a special type of encounter that I call "Locked Room." First I'll explain what it is, then I'll explain the reason behind it.

To do Locked Room, you have to replicate, as closely as you can in real life, the following set of imaginary conditions:

You and your partner are locked inside a well-ventilated but windowless room. The room does not contain a television, or radio, or telephone. There are no books, magazines, newspapers, CDs, no music of any kind—no nuthin', except for a table, two chairs, a bed, and the two of you. In short, there are *no distractions*. You do have a set of cards to play with—but no solitaire—or a set of checkers to keep you from getting completely stir-crazy. (Since it's possible to talk with each other while you play card games and checkers, they're OK.) Meals and snacks (no alcohol or drugs) are delivered to you exactly when you need them.

You and your partner are locked in this room for forty-eight hours.

Those are the conditions. You and your partner could approximate them by checking into a hotel on a Friday night and staying until Sunday night. You would not turn on the TV or radio, or make phone calls except for room service, and you wouldn't leave the room until you checked out. (You cannot do Locked Room at home. It would be too tempting not to go through with it all the way.)

The reason for doing all this is to keep the two of you in each other's presence uninterruptedly, for a long time, without the opportunity to escape. If you keep in this continuous contact, then just maybe you'll get past the point in your discussion at which you ordinarily get so nervous that one of you (or both) cuts out and the discussion aborts. You may have had this discussion many times already, but if it always aborted at the same anxiety point it's no wonder you haven't gotten anywhere. If you succeed at staying in each other's presence for a long time, long past the anxiety/abort point, you'll find that your anxiety will gradually diminish until you can deal with your very threatening agenda in a more relaxed way than you ever could before. You'll find that you come up with new ways of looking at your predicament. And you might come up with the answer that's eluded you for so long.

9. What if we *know* that we're *not* compatible in many important ways, yet we feel strongly drawn to each other and feel that we're somehow really right for each other?

Then I've got to guess that there is some kind of X-factor at work. This does happen for some couples. By "X-factor," I mean some special way that an aspect of your personality and an aspect of your partner's personality lock into each other, the way one piece of a jigsaw puzzle locks into another. That X-factor sometimes works to the detriment of the couple, as when the daughter of an alcoholic marries an alcoholic. But there are other cases where that X-factor works to the couple's benefit.

What I have in mind, especially, are instances where one of the partners (possibly both) has experienced great psychological pain and suffering. This person meets a partner with whom, for whatever reason, he or she is able to feel *safe*. And that sense of safety compensates for any incompatibilities he or she might experience with this comforting partner. Kay Redfield Jamison, in *An Unquiet Mind,* a courageous account of her struggle with manic-depression, describes such a relationship. She and the man she eventually married had strong intellectual interests in common—and for them that amounted to a shared primary concern. Aside from that, though:

> [W]e could not have been more different. . . . He was low key, I was intense; . . . he was slow to anger, I quick; the world registered gently upon him, sometimes not at all, whereas I was fast to feel both pleasure and pain. . . . Concerts and opera, mainstays of my existence, were torture to him, as were long, extended walks or vacations lasting more than three days. . . . He couldn't abide poetry [something very important to Jamison herself] and was genuinely amazed that I seemed to spend so much of my day just wandering around. [pp. 171–72]

As Jamison put it, "We were a complete mismatch." And yet:

> [N]ot once in the years we have been together have I doubted Richard's love for me, nor mine for him. . . . My life with Richard has become a safe harbor. . . . Sometimes, in the midst of one of my dreadful, destructive upheavals of mood, I feel Richard's quietness nearby and am reminded of Byron's wonderful description of the rainbow that sits "Like Hope upon a death-bed" on the verge of a wild, rushing cataract; yet, "while all around is torn / by the distracted waters" the rainbow stays serene. . . . [pp.172–75]

If you and your partner are drawn to each other by some kind of X-factor, it's important for you to identify what that factor is, if you possibly can. But by all means, take it seriously—especially if you experience that X-factor as a sense of safety. If, despite being incompatible in important ways, you still feel that rightness, that sense of safety, what else can you do but follow your heart?

13

AFTER YOU
GET MARRIED

If you and your partner have indeed gotten married, there's one thing you can say for yourselves: You have come through one of the most diabolically severe tests of your loyalty to each other that humankind has ever devised: *planning the wedding.* I congratulate you for having passed it.

I'm going to keep this chapter short because there are scores of books out there on how to be married, and some are actually helpful (and you know where you can find them listed). I'm just going to emphasize a few points that I feel haven't received enough attention.

Power Struggles: Disentangling the Concrete Issue from "Who's Right"

Power struggles happen every once in a while in all marriages, and they happen almost every day in unhappy marriages. This much has been recognized by marital therapists. What hasn't been recognized is that power struggles in marriage, whatever triggered them, are inevitably and fundamentally about Who's Right.

The issues that trigger power struggles can range all the way from small-scale ones such as "Should we go to this movie tonight, or that one?" to more consequential ones such as "Should we feed the baby now or a half hour from now?" all the way to large-scale issues where the ramifications of choosing one alternative over another are great. Most often, though, the issues are small enough in scale, and the alternatives are reasonable enough, so that things would work out fine either way. The movie we don't see tonight, we can see another night; whether we feed the baby now or later, we know she will grow up strong, healthy, and well nourished. Looked at rationally, the differences between the alternatives are too inconsequential for us to care passionately about them. So why do we sometimes get into bitter fights about them? The answer is that, even if the issue is small, we may nevertheless care passionately about being right.

There is an important connection between our passionate desire to be right and the affirmation we are getting, or not getting, in our marriage, and it is this: *The less affirmation we are getting overall from our partner, the more passionate is our desire to be right whenever we disagree with our partner.* Think of it this way: When we are in a conflict with our partner over some issue, we are not, at that moment, affirming each other. To disagree with each other and at once affirm each other is a contradiction in terms. Now, if the general level of mutual affirmation in the relationship is high (because we are compatible), then we don't have a pressing need to be affirmed over this particular issue. We are secure in the thought that our partner will be affirming us about most other things the rest of the time. As a result, shortly after the conflict slides into being a power struggle over Who's Right, or even before, we'll realize that it's OK if we're wrong, and that it doesn't matter much if the issue is decided our partner's way. We let go of the power struggle.

This is not the way things work for couples who are unhappy because of their incompatibility. For these couples, the overall level of mutual affirmation is low because the partners are too different from each other. There isn't enough mutual understanding for them to affirm each other very often. So whenever a contentious issue comes up, the partners see it as the other trying to disconfirm them and disapprove of them once more. And they each say to themselves, "They're not going to do that to me again. I'll prove to them that I'm right. *I'll* make *them affirm me.* And even if they don't, at least I'll have a chance to affirm myself right in front of their eyes." It doesn't matter how inconsequential the issue is, these unhappy partners will get into a power struggle over it because it's a chance to force the affirmation that they don't receive otherwise. That's part of the tragedy of being married to someone you're not compatible with—the lack of mutual affirmation leads to unremitting, bitter power struggles.

The moral of the story, for your *happy* marriage, is that as soon as you become aware that the two of you are in a power struggle, you can just let go of it. You know that you're getting lots of affirmation most of the time, so you don't have to have it all the time. An easy way of signifying to your partner that you're letting go of the power struggle is to suggest that you flip a coin about the issue. (My belief is that if coins weren't made specifically for flipping they would never have been invented, and we'd be getting along just fine—better—with paper money.) When your partner agrees to the coin flip, that means that you have both agreed to disentangle the concrete issue from Who's Right. And as soon as you do that, the conflict is instantly resolved. What you must do, then, is to be on the lookout for the point at which conflict slides into being a power struggle over Who's Right, and immediately sound the alarm by suggesting, "Hey, let's just flip a coin."

HisWay/HerWay

There are some issues, though, that no one in their right mind would decide by a coin flip. Those are issues that commit each of you to a particular pattern of behavior for a long time. You simply must come to some agreement about them. The problem is that it's as easy, easier even, to get into power struggles over Who's Right on these issues than on less consequential ones. The paradox is that the more you try to "negotiate" them, the deeper you dig yourself into the power struggle over Who's Right. There must be a better way.

There is, because I invented it. I call it "HisWay/HerWay." You can use HisWay/HerWay after you're married, but it also can be useful in helping you before you get married. HisWay/HerWay can help you come to agreements on aspects of your day-to-day life that you identified as points of disagreement along the Practical Dimension and occasionally it can even be useful for disagreements on the Wavelength Dimension, in instances when those disagreements involve the conduct of your daily life. First I'll give a case example of HisWay/HerWay (of the first time it occurred to me to use it, actually), then I'll explain how it works, and then I'll give another example, of a premarital case.

Beverly and Phil were a lovely couple in their late twenties. They'd been married for about five years and it was immediately evident that they had a strong bond. Underneath all the anger and frustration, they respected each other—they loved each other. (They were one of those "good-gut" couples.) Nevertheless, the conflict between them over the past few months had become so severe that they'd sought me out. The conflict boiled down to the fact that each had habits that drove the other crazy.

Phil was a concrete contractor, pouring foundations and the like. The two habits of his that drove Beverly crazy were: (1) When he came home from work, he'd walk through the house in his boots, leaving deposits of hardened mud and cement everywhere; (2) He always did his estimating in the evening, right after the day's construction work was over, so he was almost never home for dinner on workdays. Beverly was a high school teacher, but her great passion—her primary concern, which Phil did share to an extent—was dogs. As part of this passion, Beverly was heavily involved in what is called "greyhound rescue." Whenever her rescue organization found out about unwanted greyhounds, whether dogs in pounds or dogs about to be disposed of (killed, that is) by dog-racing tracks, members of the group would take the dogs into their homes until people could be found who would adopt them. Beverly had crates (large individual cages) to accommodate four dogs, and at any given time there were two to four dogs in residence. Phil didn't mind the dogs, he minded the mess. No, not the dogs' mess—they were pretty neat. He minded Beverly's mess. Evidently, greyhound rescue involves a lot of paperwork, and Beverly had littered the whole house with doggie documentation. Most of the surface of the dining room table was covered with piles of it. All that paper drove Phil nuts.

After listening for some minutes to both of them trying to convince me that they were right, I got my brainstorm and said, "I wonder what it would be like if, for two weeks, all decisions great and small [except, as I added later, for sex, which must always be consensual] went your way, and then if they all went *your* way for the two weeks after that." I explained what I meant. First, they would have to buy into this experiment. In other words, they each would pledge to abide by the other's wishes—right now, even before knowing exactly what the other might demand of them. Then, whoever went first, having it his or her way, would stipulate what he or she wanted of the other for that two-week period. This would *not* be a negotiation. The person who was having it his or her way would just tell the other partner what he or she wanted, and the other partner would just say yes and do it. Both could demand what they wanted about anything, for example, that they go to bed no later than 10:00 P.M. or that they not watch TV for those two weeks—anything. With respect to the specific issues that triggered their power struggle, Beverly could rule that Phil would have to be home for dinner by 5:30 P.M. every night of the week, or that he leave his work boots outside the house before walking in. Phil could demand that Beverly remove every scrap of greyhound documentation from the house, or not accept any new dogs over the coming two weeks—anything, as long as it did not commit Beverly to doing anything that would extend beyond Phil's two weeks.

I then asked them if they were sure—sure they were sure—they were willing to buy into the HisWay/HerWay experiment. After some questions and further discussion they said, with some obvious trepidation, that they were.

The results of the experiment were as follows: When it was HerWay, Beverly asked that Phil come home by 7:00 P.M. three nights out of the workweek, and she asked that he enter the house by the back door and go no farther than the back entryway before removing his boots. When it was HisWay, Phil asked only that Beverly keep the dining room table and the living room free of greyhound papers. Both Phil and Beverly, when it was their partner's way, abided with their partner's wishes 100 percent, and they didn't find it hard to do. After the HisWay/HerWay experiment, this particular power struggle in their marriage disappeared.

Why did HisWay/HerWay work for Beverly and Phil? It worked, first of all, by separating out the issues from the power struggle over Who's Right. Once Beverly and Phil bought into the experiment, they were agreeing to act according to their partner's preferences—but not because their partner had somehow forced them to, or because their partner was right. They were going to act according to their partner's wishes *of their own free will*, simply because they'd bought into the experiment. They could continue to think whatever they wanted to about their partner being wrong, but they were going to act *as if* their partner were right. And, whether they realized it or not, Beverly and Phil were also tacitly acknowledging that their partner's requirements would not be so extreme as to be impossible to fulfill.

HisWay/HerWay also worked by reaffirming Phil's and Beverly's trust in each other. Just by agreeing to the experiment, they were acknowledging that they felt safe about putting themselves entirely in the other's hands. And then each of them demonstrated their own trustworthiness, in two ways. First, they each complied with the other's wishes 100 percent. Second, when it was their turn to have the power, neither of them made extreme demands: Beverly didn't ask Phil to come home at 5:30 every day, and Phil didn't require Beverly to get all the papers out of the kitchen and the other rooms in the house, or not to take in any dogs. Being in the HisWay/HerWay experiment enabled Beverly and Phil to limit themselves to moderate demands, specifically because HisWay/HerWay disentangled the concrete issues from the power struggle. Once Beverly and Phil were disconnected from that struggle, they could move back closer to each other, back from the extreme positions that the struggle had polarized them into. When they saw that the other wasn't power tripping them, *even though that would have been allowed by the experiment,* each felt safer about hearing the other's preferences and accommodating them.

That's how I think HisWay/HerWay works. Now for the premarital example.

Even though Ben and Jessica were only in their late twenties, they had both been married before—miserably—and divorced. Both had been hurt in their previous marriage, and this time they had each taken pains to choose the right person. My sense was that, overall, they had succeeded. They were referred to me because, although they were well matched with each other, there were still "a few issues" to work out. But these "few issues" included a big one: conflict over the Jewish dietary laws—kashruth.

As you may know, observing kashruth involves a number of different things: not eating pork products; not eating shellfish; eating meat only from animals that have been ritually slaughtered, in a way that, according to tradition, minimizes the animal's suffering and honors the animal's life even as it is being taken; and not mixing milk products with meat, either in cooking or in eating. Some Jews observe these laws to the letter, going as far, for example, as having separate sets of pots, dishes, and flatware for meat meals and dairy meals. Other Jews don't observe them at all. Some others observe them partially, for example, eating pork and shellfish in restaurants but never at home.

It was Ben and Jessica's bad luck to be at opposite poles on kashruth. Ben had grown up in an Orthodox home in a small town in New Jersey where almost all the Jews were Orthodox. Keeping kosher was important to him. (He'd made a few forays into the nonkosher world during his rebellious youth, but now that he was getting married again he wanted a kosher home.) Jessica had grown up in a well-to-do Reform Jewish family on New York's sophisticated Upper East Side. Her family had never kept kosher. She told me her favorite food was calamari. Big problem.

Jessica and Ben had the kinds of heated, self-righteous fights over Who's Right that people can have only about religion: "It's so old-fashioned and pointless to keep kosher." "But it's our tradition." "We now know that we won't get trichinosis from eating pork." "That's not the point. The point is that being kosher is how you show everyone else, and yourself—not to mention God—that you're Jewish." "There are lots of other ways to be Jewish without keeping kosher. I'm sure that God will understand."

Nasty stuff like that. It was clear with this couple, as with Phil and Beverly, that more "negotiation" about this issue would get them exactly nowhere. So I explained HisWay/HerWay to them, and they were willing to try it. They handled the experiment differently from Phil and Beverly, but the final result was the same. Ben and Jessica demanded more of each other than Phil and Beverly had. Ben, for example, required that Jessica keep kosher even when he wasn't around, for example, when she went out to lunch with her friends. Jessica demanded that Ben eat some nonkosher food. As they later told me, both had been expecting that their partner would not abide by their wishes—that is, not live up to the deal they had made. They were both wrong. Ben did eat the nonkosher dishes that Jessica put in front of him, and Jessica did keep kosher even when Ben wasn't around. The fact that each was willing to abide by the other's wishes, if only for the two weeks of the experiment, was surprising to both of them. And it was deeply reassuring because it demonstrated that they were each capable of much more flexibility than either of them had manifested before.

After HisWay/HerWay, kashruth ceased to be an issue for Ben and Jessica. The experience of agreeing to live according to the other's kashruth standard for a short time freed them to create a joint standard that they both could live with over the long term. (A couple of years later, Ben told me he felt that HisWay/HerWay had also helped him better deal with Jessica's family on issues connected with observance of Jewish holidays.) HisWay/HerWay helped Ben and Jessica in the same way it did Beverly and Phil: first by disentangling the concrete issue from the struggle over Who's Right, and then by reaffirming their trust in each other.

As these two examples show, you can use HisWay/HerWay as a way to stop power struggles and come to agreement, either before you get married or after. It's just a matter of being aware, as early as possible, of the issues that are most likely to cause those struggles. Give HisWay/HerWay a try, if the opportunity arises, and then let me know how it came out.

The Long Conversation

People say that negotiation is important in marriage. They say that when a big issue comes up, one in which you and your partner have opposing interests, you must negotiate. You have to give a little, your partner has to give a little; you compromise. But what happy couples do to solve their biggest problems is not negotiation. And the solutions they finally arrive at are not compromises. The solutions of happy couples are, literally, re-visions—a whole, new, shared vision of what their life together is and of what it can be. And the way they arrive at these re-visions is what I call the "Long Conversation."

What happily married people do is not negotiation for one simple reason: They love each other and care about each other. In fact, it is exactly this element of love and caring that is missing in ordinary negotiation—and that makes negotiation necessary.

Think about yourself and a car salesman. You're trying to buy the car for the lowest possible price, and he's trying to sell it to you for the highest possible price. You don't have his best interest in mind and he doesn't have yours in mind—and there's no reason that either of you should. You are strangers to each other. You probably will never see each other again after this transaction. You certainly don't love each other. There is no good reason for either of you to care about the other's welfare. We all know this and accept this. You may try to use good-faith negotiating techniques to get to a "win-win" outcome. But that's only because you care about you, not because you care about the salesman. You don't.

We do love the person we married. And we do care, deeply, about that person. Because of that love and caring, we don't hunker down into a hardheaded negotiation when a situation arises where we disagree, or where our interests, in some important way, are opposed. We'd like to get what we individually want, naturally, but not at the price of hurting this person we love. So what we do is embark on the Long Conversation.

The Long Conversation is not a negotiation, although it may contain elements of that from time to time. The Long Conversation is actually focusing. It is an extended, joint focusing session in which we go through a process of emotional unfolding together. By way of this emotional unfolding, we eventually arrive at a point where suddenly we see a new way of going on together that will be OK for both of us.

There is a trail that begins at Muir Woods National Monument, in California. I think it is the Ben Jonson Trail. You start in the valley among the towering redwoods, and you hike uphill. The trail is all uphill. Before too long, the trail gets boring. You're hot, you're sweaty, you're wondering how much more of this there is. You keep on hiking uphill. Suddenly, without warning, you find yourself out of the woods, on a high, grassy meadow, with a cool breeze in your face. You are looking out over the Pacific. That's what the Long Conversation feels like, and what it feels like when the two of you arrive at that new vision of your life together. You may not be able to describe exactly how you got to that new vision, just as you couldn't describe exactly how the Ben Jonson Trail got you to the Pacific. All you know is that the Long Conversation got you there.

When I say the Long Conversation, I mean *long*. It lasts not just a couple or three hours, it lasts many hours. It goes on not for just an hour or two at a time, it goes on for three or five or eight hours at a time. Or longer. You go on very long walks or take very long drives. The main thing is that you stay in each other's presence to get you through the anxiety that comes from having to talk with each other about something that is at once very big and very perplexing. You don't get past all the anxiety, just enough of it so that you can start to feel something else alongside it.[1] You talk, and then you keep on talking. It gets boring. You seem to be rehashing the same stuff, saying the very same sentences over and over again. Nothing seems to be happening. But something is happening—that process of emotional unfolding inside each of you. You keep on talking, and keep on being bored and frustrated. Sometimes you get angry at each other, sometimes you're just despairing. And there are periods in the Long Conversation when neither of you is saying anything. You're walking or driving together, and you're both too weary to say anything, and you don't know what to say. But all this while your emotional unfolding continues deep inside you. At some moment that you can't predict you begin to feel the breeze on your face and get your first glimpse of the ocean.

In chapter 6, I mentioned the tough decision that Sue and I had to make about whether to pick up and move to Chicago or stay in New Jersey. When Sue first got the phone call, her initial reaction, and mine, was denial. We refused to believe that the job offer was real. It was not in writing, it would probably get stopped at higher levels—or so we wanted to think. But then, three months later, when the letter did come, we couldn't deny it anymore: We had a problem. My initial reaction was that I wanted Sue to take the job because it was a wonderful opportunity for her—but I couldn't possibly make the move myself. It was not simply the dreadful prospect of having to close my practice and start over again, from ground zero, in Chicago. It was everything I'd have to leave: my mother and brother, who live in New York, the house in New Jersey that I'd come to love (including the pine trees I'd always wanted, and had planted with my own hands), my patients, my great friends Tim and Paul, even the New York disc jockeys whom I'd come to love as friends—

everyone from David Garland on WNYC to Cousin Brucie on WCBS. I couldn't imagine—literally, I could not visualize—being cut off from all this. And I couldn't visualize anything good about Chicago, a place I'd never been to and that had never held any particular interest for me.

Sue, meanwhile, was in terrible emotional turmoil herself. Part of her really wanted to take the job at the University of Chicago, and she had utter faith in my ability to start over again. But she felt enormously guilty about how much I'd miss all the things I loved about my life in New Jersey, and how I'd grieve over them. And she felt guilty about putting me through all the troubles I would certainly have in starting my professional life over, even if I did succeed in the end. And we were both very concerned about tearing our daughter away from her friends and from the only place she'd ever lived.

In our perplexity and anxiety, Sue and I did the only thing we could do. We embarked on the Long Conversation. I cannot say that the following ten months were easy. As we continued, and continued, our Long Conversation, there were many moments when we were tense, and when we were angry and nasty to each other. There were many occasions when we did not follow the principles of good marital communication. We're only human, all of us, and no one is nice all the time when they are in the midst of the Long Conversation. There were many times on our long walks and long drives when we said nothing at all. But all the while the emotional unfolding was going on in each of us, and by sometime in the ninth month I began to get glimpses of how it could be OK to leave the things I loved and move to Chicago. And Sue got glimpses of how her acceptance of the U of C's offer didn't have to be an irrevocable decision. She could see it as tentative, as a trial, something she could ultimately say no to if things weren't working out for *us*. Sue and I now know that things did work out, but we didn't know that then. All we knew was that we would both be OK with whatever happened—whether we stayed in Chicago, returned to New Jersey, or did something else altogether.

The Long Conversation doesn't necessarily last as long as nine or ten months. It could last a day or two, or it could last longer than ten months, depending on the scale and the complexity of the decision before you.

But, however long it takes, the Long Conversation is not a negotiation. It doesn't feel like sitting at opposite sides of a table. It feels like sitting next to each other.

THERE'S ONE more thing I want to say before ending this book, something about how it feels to be in a happy marriage. No, not love. Something bigger, more encompassing than love.

14

DEVOTION

Living for you
Is easy living
It's easy to live
When you're in love
And I'm so in love
There's nothing in life but you . . .

I'll never regret
The things I'm giving
They're easy to give
When you're in love
I'm happy to do
Whatever I do for you.

—from *Easy Living*

Someone in Your Corner

Have you ever seen a prizefight? I've seen some. If you can't form a clear and detailed image of a prizefight, rent a movie about prizefighting— *Rocky* or *Raging Bull*. Watch as much as you can of what happens during the rounds, what the fighters do to each other. Watch especially what happens between the rounds: When the round ends, each fighter returns to his corner, and there's someone in his corner.

For many of us, life is like a prizefight, too much like a prizefight. We leave our corner and we are faced with brutal competition, hostility, and aggression. Even if we don't want a fight, we have no choice about it. We are forced to defend ourselves—which means hitting back, too. It's like a prizefight, only there aren't any rules to keep it fair, and there isn't a referee in there to make sure we don't get hit below the belt. Sometimes our opponent is bigger and stronger than we are, and we get badly beaten.

For some of us, there's someone waiting for us when we get back to our corner. They're not in the ring with us. We fight our own fight. But they're waiting in our corner. They wipe the sweat from our face. They put something on the cut that's opened up over our eye. They give us a sip of water. They tell us we can do it. They prod us when we are not fighting hard enough. When the fight is over, and our whole body is hurt, and we've lost, they tell us we'll win next time.

If you are in a happy marriage, you feel—you *know*—that there's someone in your corner. They don't fight the fight for you—you fight your fight yourself—but they're waiting in your corner to help you between rounds, and to help you after the fight is over. They're in your corner to reassure you that even though you're out there in the ring by yourself, you're not alone. They're in your corner no matter what, even if they're impatient with you, exasperated with you, enraged at you. They are always in your corner.

Devotion

Your partner is in your corner, always, and you are in your partner's corner, always, out of *devotion*. Not commitment, devotion.

Commitment is what keeps us doing the things we *must* do, the things we've *pledged* to do. Commitment is why people will run twenty blocks to make it on time for an appointment, or work day and night to meet a deadline, or pay back a debt even though they have barely enough to survive. If we are committed enough, we will do what we pledged to do no matter how undermining, no matter how catastrophic, it may be to our own personal welfare. Commitment is why some people remain forever in their unhappy marriage, through decades of "hard work," decades of gritted teeth.

Devotion is why people in a happy marriage do what they do for each other and give what they give to each other. They do those things and give those things willingly, joyfully. As the old song says, "They're easy to give when you're in love."

The dictionary doesn't even use the word "love" when it defines devotion. It just says, "loyalty, faithfulness, deep affection." Love is something you feel, or say you feel. Love is something that people say but don't feel. Devotion is not something you say. It is something you do. You *do* devotion, and you keep on doing it; it's out there, concrete and visible, for all the world to see.

Devotion is when you keep on giving, even after you have been released from your pledge. And so, Ida Strauss stepped away from her lifeboat and back on to the *Titanic,* telling her husband, "We have been living together for many years and where you go, I go." And she stayed with him, as the ship went down, lying next to him in their stateroom, in bed.

It is devotion you feel, devotion you do, if you are blessed with a happy marriage.

I do not know if I believe in Marriage, but I do know that I believe in *marriages*. I believe in the marriages of my family and friends: Steve and Toni, Debbie and Paul, Susan and Mark, Tim and Eileen, Mary Alice and Gene, Steven and Bonnie. I believe in the marriage of Sue's parents. I believe in my own marriage, with Sue. It is the most important, the happiest fact of my life. I believe in all the different marriages in which compatibility generates lasting love. I wish you a marriage you can believe in: a marriage of mutual understanding, affirmation, and respect; a marriage in which your love lasts because, from day to day, from moment to moment, you and your partner create new love. I wish you a marriage of devotion.

Endnotes

CHAPTER 1 *The Question: What Makes Marriages Happy?*

1. Vincent, J. P., Weiss, R. L., and Birchler, G. R., "A behavioral analysis of problem solving in distressed and nondistressed married and stranger dyads," *Behavior Therapy* 6, pp. 475–87, 1975.

2. Behavioral marital therapy (BMT) has been more thoroughly studied than any other approach to marital therapy. BMT generally includes a good deal of direct training in communication and problem solving, plus techniques to increase positive exchange between the spouses. A review of outcome studies of BMT revealed that only half the client couples improved enough by the end of treatment to be classified as "nondistressed," and that for some of these couples the improvement had disappeared when they were followed up a year later. There is no reason to suppose that any of the approaches to marital therapy that have not been tested are any more effective than BMT. (See Johnson, N. S., and

Addis, M. E., "Research on couples and couple therapy: What do we know? Where are we going?" *Journal of Consulting and Clinical Psychology* 61, pp. 85–93, 1993.

CHAPTER 2 *The Answer: Compatibility*

1. Emotional intelligence is very important to success and happiness in life. Read all about it in *Emotional Intelligence: Why It Can Matter More Than IQ*, by Daniel Goleman (New York: Bantam, 1995).

2. See, for example, *Acceptance and Change in Couple Therapy: A Therapist's Guide to Transforming Relationships*, by Neil S. Jacobson and Andrew Christensen (New York: Norton, 1998).

3. See *Uncoupling: Turning Points in Intimate Relationships*, by Diane Vaughan (New York: Vintage, 1990) for many such examples.

CHAPTER 3 *How Love Fits In*

1. Of course, if at any point you do not like what you are discovering you don't let yourself fall into romantic love. Your readiness for romantic love, which was switched on by initial sexual attraction, is switched off. And then either you don't pursue the relationship any further, or you define it as some other kind of relationship—a friendly but noncommitted erotic relationship, for example.

CHAPTER 6 *Filling In the Details: Your (My) Questions Answered*

1. This example can be found in Christensen, A., and Walczynski, P. T., "Conflict and Satisfaction in Couples," in R. J. Sternberg and M. Hojjat (eds.), *Satisfaction in Close Relationships* (New York: Guilford Press, 1997), p. 255. In this chapter, as in his other books, Christensen asserts that most incompatibilities are brought into the marriage by the partners. He concedes that it's possible that incompatibilities can develop sometimes, and this is the example.

2. Rutgers did not make the top twenty, in rankings done by the National Research Council. See Honan, W. H., "Study of Graduate Student Programs Serves up Some Surprises," *The New York Times*, September 13, 1995, p. A-8.

3. For a brief review of the literature on human resilience in the face of childhood trauma and adversity see pages 387–89 of a paper by yours truly, "Learned

Helplessness Leads to Inherited Hypohedonia: A Conjecture Updated," *Review of General Psychology*, 2, 1998, pp. 384–403.

4. Mavis Hetherington of the University of Virginia is the authority. You can find this quote on page 170 of an article written by her and two colleagues: "What Matters? What Does Not? Five Perspectives on the Association Between Marital Transitions and Children's Adjustment," *American Psychologist*, 53, February 1998, pp. 167–84. Although this is an article in a professional journal, it is not that technical; and if you are a child of divorce or the parent of one, reading it will be a reassuring experience.

5. As you might have guessed, this quote is from John Gray's *Men Are from Mars, Women Are from Venus* (New York: HarperCollins, 1992), p. 5.

6. See *Sex and Gender Differences in Personal Relationships*, by Daniel J. Canary and Tara M. Emmers-Sommer (New York: Guilford Press, 1997), for a comprehensive review of the scientific studies on this subject.

7. Again, see *Sex and Gender Differences in Personal Relationships*, by Canary and Emmers-Sommer, for a review of these studies.

CHAPTER 7 *Avoiding Bad News*

1. Culligan, J. J., *When in Doubt Check Him Out: A Woman's Survival Guide for the 90s* (Miami, FL: Hallmark Press, 1997).

2. Holtzworth-Monroe, A., Beatty, S. B., and Anglin, K., "The Assessment and Treatment of Marital Violence: An Introduction for the Marital Therapist," in N. S. Jacobson and A. S. Gurman (eds.), *Clinical Handbook of Marital Therapy* (New York: Guilford Press, 1995), p. 334.

3. Bok, S., *Lying: Moral Choice in Public and Private Life* (New York: Vintage, 1989). This a great, potentially life-changing book.

CHAPTER 8 *Feeling Your Compatibility*

1. Gendlin, E. T., *Focusing* (New York: Bantam, 1981).

CHAPTER 9 *The Practical Dimension*

1. This classification of marriages roughly follows that presented by Pepper Schwartz in her book, *Love Between Equals* (New York: The Free Press, 1995).

2. See *The Second Shift* by Arlie Hochschild and Anne Machung (New York: Viking, 1989) for an account of the nature and consequences of this kind of arrangement.

3. See *America: What Went Wrong?* by Donald L. Barlett and James B. Steele (Andrews McNeel Publishing, 1992) for more information about this and other economic trends over the past half-century.

4. Since spending priorities are so closely bound up with values, I could have included them in the Wavelength Dimension. I included them in the Practical Dimension simply because they involve concrete, practical decisions that come up almost daily. You've probably realized by now that the three compatibility dimensions are not completely separate from one another. As a professor of mine in graduate school once said, "Rule Number One of psychology is that everything is related to everything else."

5. This story appeared in a Boston newspaper but I heard it much earlier, from Marilee's mother.

6. In case you were wondering, a couple of the other neat tricks of happy marriage are (a) staying separate enough from each other while maintaining togetherness; and (b) staying sexually alive while remaining monogamous.

CHAPTER 10 *The Sexual Dimension*

1. A pioneering woman gynecologist—she was old in the 1960s—told this story: She'd advised a young college coed that, for birth control, she should consider a diaphragm and spermicidal jelly. The coed replied, "But that's messy." The doctor replied, "My dear, sex is messy."

2. *The Rake's Progress*—music by Igor Stravinsky, libretto by W. H. Auden and Chester Kallman.

3. Another "if-I-had-a-nickel-for-every" category: a man who marries a woman with whom the sex is not as passionate as he had experienced with others, because he thinks (often rightly) that this woman will be a good mother.

CHAPTER 11 *The Wavelength Dimension*

1. Orwall, B., and Lublin, J. S., "Disney Chief's Exercise of Stock Options Irks Some Investors, but Street Is Calm," *The Wall Street Journal*, December 5, 1997, p. A-4.

2. Charlie Parker (1920–1955) was an alto saxophonist and jazz innovator. One

of the creators of the modern jazz (or "bebop") style in the 1940s, he was *the* stylistic influence for players of all instruments for the next two decades or so, and remains a major influence for all jazz musicians.

CHAPTER 12 *Yikes! What Do We Do Now?* *And Your (My) Other Questions Answered*

1. Information on PREPARE, including information on counselors near you who administer it, can be obtained from Life Innovations, Inc., PO Box 190, Minneapolis, MN 55440-0190; phone 800-331-1661.

CHAPTER 13 *After You Get Married*

1. Yes, Locked Room is a compressed form of the Long Conversation.

For Further Reading

Reconcilable Differences, by Andrew Christensen and Neil S. Jacobson. New York: Guilford Press, 2000.

This book helps partners resolve conflict by enabling them to acknowledge and accept their incompatibilities. The authors present a number of creative methods for promoting acceptance, and for stopping destructive patterns stemming from partners' desire to change each other. The authors' understanding of marriage and marital problems is very similar to the one I've presented in this book.

The Power of Two, by Susan Heitler. Oakland, Calif.: New Harbinger Press, 1998.

This book is very easy to use and packed with detailed, useful information. It has many exercises to help couples learn how to communicate in more constructive ways. Especially useful are the contrasting conversations that show the differences between a couple with good communication habits and a couple with bad communication habits.

Fighting for Your Marriage: Positive Steps for Preventing Divorce and Preserving Lasting Love, by Howard J. Markman, Scott M. Stanley, and Susan L. Blumberg. San Francisco: Jossey-Bass, 1996.

Markman has done research on couples' interaction patterns. This book is based partly on that research and on a marital-enhancement program that he and his colleagues developed and tested.

For Each Other: Sharing Sexual Intimacy, by Lonnie Barbach. New York: Signet, 1984.

An excellent book on female sexuality.

The New Male Sexuality: The Truth About Men, Sex, and Pleasure, by Bernie Zilbergeld. New York: Bantam, 1999.

Very informative and also very funny.

How to Win as a Step-Family, 2nd edition, by Emily B. Visher and John S. Visher. New York: Brunner-Mazel, 1991.

An excellent book on stepparenting and blended-family issues.

Permissions

From *Men Are from Mars, Women Are from Venus* by John Gray, © 1992 by John Gray. Reprinted with permission from HarperCollins Publishers.

From *Easy Living* by Leo Robin and Ralph Rainger, © 1937 by Famous Music Corporation, © renewed 1964 by Famous Music Corporation.

From *Satisfaction in Close Relationships* edited by R. J. Sternberg and M. Hojjat, © 1997 by Robert J. Sternberg and Mahzad Hojjat. Reprinted with permission from Guilford Press.

From *Into Thin Air* by Jon Krakauer, © 1997 by Jon Krakauer. Reprinted with permission from Villard.

From *An Unquiet Mind* by Kay Redfield Jamison, © 1995 by Kay Redfield Jamison. Reprinted with permission from Alfred Knopf.

About the Author

Sam R. Hamburg, Ph.D., is a clinical psychologist and marital therapist in private practice. He is a lecturer in the Department of Psychiatry of Pritzker School of Medicine, The University of Chicago, and is a member of the adjunct faculty of The Family Institute at Northwestern University. Dr. Hamburg is also on the executive committee of the Marjorie Kovler Center for the Treatment of Survivors of Torture, an agency that offers pro bono psychotherapy and rehabilitation to individuals who have been subjected to torture and other traumatic events. Dr. Hamburg, his wife, and their daughter live in Chicago.

Dr. Hamburg welcomes your comments and questions. You can reach him at his Web site:

www.willourlovelast.com

About the Illustrator

Gene Mackay is an artist and museum designer. His work is in the collections of the Rochester Museum and the New York State Museum, and has been exhibited at the White House.